A gift from:
Friends of the
Pinole Library

EXPLORERS
AND
EXPLORATION

1

ALEXANDER THE GREAT — BELL, GERTRUDE

Marshall Cavendish

New York • London • Singapore

Marshall Cavendish
99 White Plains Road
Tarrytown, New York 10591-9001

www.marshallcavendish.com

Consultants: Ralph Ehrenberg, former chief, Geography
and Map Division, Library of Congress, Washington, DC;
Conrad Heidenreich, former historical geography
professor, York University, Toronto; Shane Winser,
information officer, Royal Geographical Society, London

Contributing authors: Dale Anderson, Kay Barnham,
Peter Chrisp, Richard Dargie, Paul Dowswell, Elizabeth
Gogerly, Steven Maddocks, John Malam, Stewart Ross,
Shane Winser

MARSHALL CAVENDISH
Editor: Thomas McCarthy
Editorial Director: Paul Bernabeo
Production Manager: Michael Esposito

WHITE-THOMSON PUBLISHING
Editors: Alex Woolf and Steven Maddocks
Design: Ross George and Derek Lee
Cartographer: Peter Bull Design
Picture Research: Glass Onion Pictures
Indexer: Fiona Barr

ISBN 0-7614-7535-4 (set)

ISBN 0-7614-7536-2 (vol. 1)

Printed in China

08 07 06 05 04   5 4 3 2 1

Library of Congress Cataloging-in-Publication Data
Explorers and exploration.
    p. cm.
  Includes bibliographical references (p.   ) and index.
  ISBN 0-7614-7535-4 (set : alk. paper) -- ISBN 0-7614-
7536-2 (v. 1) -- ISBN 0-7614-7537-0 (v. 2) -- ISBN 0-7614-
7538-9 (v. 3) -- ISBN 0-7614-7539-7 (v. 4) -- ISBN 0-7614-
7540-0 (v. 5) -- ISBN 0-7614-7541-9 (v. 6) -- ISBN 0-7614-
7542-7 (v. 7) -- ISBN 0-7614-7543-5 (v. 8) -- ISBN 0-7614-
7544-3 (v. 9) -- ISBN 0-7614-7545-1 (v. 10) -- ISBN 0-
7614-7546-X (v. 11)
  1. Explorers--Encyclopedias. 2. Discoveries in
geography--Encyclopedias. I. Marshall Cavendish
Corporation. II. Title.
  G80.E95 2005
  910'.92'2--dc22

                    2004048292

ILLUSTRATION CREDITS

AKG London: 15 (Alte Pinakothek, Munich), 22, 51
(AKG / Nimatallah), 59, 71 (Fogg Art Museum,
Cambridge, Mass.).

Bridgeman Art Library: 14 (Louvre, Paris), 17, 21, 44
(Royal Society, London), 45 (Museo di Storia della
Scienza, Florence), 49 (Bibliothèque Nationale, Paris), 53
(Musée de la Tapisserie, Bayeux, France), 55 (New York
Historical Society), 56 (Victoria and Albert Museum,
London), 61 (Archives Charmet), 69 (Ken Welsh), 70.

Corbis: 24, 25 (Bettman / Corbis).

Gertrude Bell Photographic Archive: 76, 77, 78.

Mary Evans Picture Library: 18, 19, 62, 68.

Missouri Historical Society: 30.

Peter Newark's American Pictures: 26, 31, 32, 34, 75.

Peter Newark's Pictures: 20.

Popperfoto: 29, 33, 36, 39, 42.

Science and Society Picture Library: 67.

Science Photo Library: 27, 28 (NASA), 37 (NOVOSTI),
38, 40, 41 (NASA), 43, 46 (David Nunuk), 47 (NASA), 48
(European Space Agency), 50 (Alfred Pasieka), 52 (Allan
Morton / Dennis Milon), 54 (Dr. Seth Shostak), 64 (Dr.
Morley Read), 65 (NASA).

Topham Picturepoint: 23, 60, 72, 73.

Cover: Ptolemaic armillary sphere, 1648 (Bridgeman
Art Library / Science Museum, London).

color key	time period
▬▬▬	to 500
▬▬▬	500–1400
▬▬▬	1400–1850
▬▬▬	1850–1945
▬▬▬	1945–2000
▬▬▬	general articles

Set Contents

VOLUME 10

VOLUME 11

THEMATIC CONTENTS

This thematic table of contents organizes the articles in this encyclopedia into five major sections. One of the sections, People, is further divided into several subsections. Within each section and subsection, article titles are organized alphabetically; certain article titles appear in more than one place. For each page listing, the number that precedes the colon is the volume number.

PEOPLE

INSTITUTIONS

SCIENCE AND TECHNOLOGY

GENERAL ARTICLES

INTRODUCTION

The knowledge of the world that people now enjoy is the culmination of more than two millennia of human endeavor. These volumes tell the story of that endeavor, a story that has false starts as well as great achievements and terrible tragedies as well as feats of inspiring heroism. The explorer reaches into the unknown, whether through the invention of a new technology, the introduction of a new method of navigation, or the discovery of a new land. For the student, the history of exploration serves as an index of the history of human civilization. These volumes tell of many moments when, to paraphrase Neil Armstrong, the small steps of a lone man or woman were great leaps for humankind.

Explorers have been inspired by motives both noble and base. Many were tempted to brave the unknown by the profits to be made from the sale of silk, spices, precious metals, furs, and exotic goods. Some were enticed by legends to search for islands of silver, cities of gold, and even a whole continent—*Terra Australis,* the southern landmass—that did not exist.

During the Age of Exploration, which began in the fifteenth century, the finding of a new land, especially one whose inhabitants lacked significant military power, was often seen by European nations as an opportunity for territorial expansion and economic enrichment. Many explorers were instructed to claim the lands they found for the government that sponsored them. Where native peoples contested a claim, land might be taken by conquest, a process that often (but not invariably) had devastating results for the conquered peoples. Church authorities saw in the new discoveries an opportunity to extend the bounds of Christendom, not by conquest but by conversion of native peoples. Whether aggressive or not, however, the first encounters between European explorers and native peoples of the Americas, Africa, and Australia brought about significant and permanent changes in human culture and civilization.

The aims of some explorers and expeditions were intellectual, at least in part. The surveying of the continents, the conquest of the Poles, and even the search for the Northwest and Northeast Passages were, to some extent, exploration for its own sake. In the nineteenth century, widespread interest in anthropology, botany, and zoology inspired many to venture in search of specimens. Soon huge collections of artifacts, plants, and fossils were being displayed and studied in the great museums of Europe and the United States.

No study of the history of exploration would be complete without period maps. Those reproduced in these pages range from an Egyptian papyrus of 1150 BCE to twenty-first-century satellite images. A map is a visual corollary to the story of exploration; in what it gets wrong as much as what it gets right, it reveals the sum of geographical knowledge at any given moment in history.

The story of exploration is by no means a closed book. Underwater, underground, and in space are unexplored regions and unexplained mysteries. Through television and the Internet the world will share, as never before, in the next small steps and great leaps forward in knowledge of the world and, beyond, of the universe.

Shane Winser

Expedition Advisory Centre, Royal Geographical Society

READER'S GUIDE

This encyclopedia contains a total of 177 articles in ten volumes, articles that cover the entire history of exploration from ancient times to the present day. The articles fall into one or another of the following five categories: people; places; institutions; science and technology; and general articles. The Thematic Contents, found on pages 8 to 11 in this volume, organizes the articles under these headings.

All articles contain at least one informational display, or panel. There are four types of panels in total. Fact panels highlight matters of exceptional interest in the subject under discussion. Technology panels describe particular aspects or items of technology used by explorers or expeditions. Biographical panels offer brief accounts of significant individuals not covered in the main articles; birth and death dates, where known, are included alongside each individual's name. Quotation panels provide illuminating quotes from contemporary sources.

For ease of reference, articles have been color-coded by time period (general articles have a color code of their own). The codes, which may be found at the front of each volume, are as follows:

Virtually all articles include a list of key dates, and articles about specific journeys include a map. Every article concludes with a list of cross-references to other, related articles.

Each volume concludes with a glossary and an index. Volume 11, the final volume, contains a time line of exploration, a comprehensive glossary, resources for further study, Internet resources, a map list and index, a group of thematic indexes, and a comprehensive index.

to 500 CE

500–1400

1400–1850

1850–1945

1945–2000

general articles

The color code indicates which period of history corresponds with the subject of the article.

All articles about journeys contain a map.

Technology panels give details of the technology or equipment used on particular journeys.

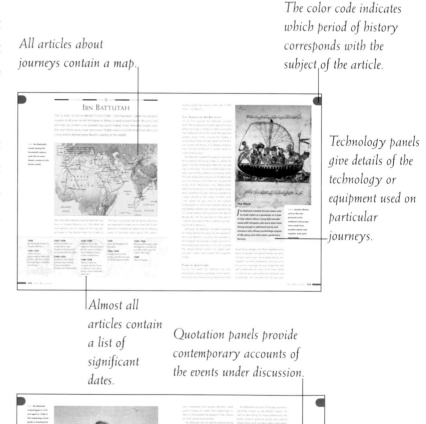

Almost all articles contain a list of significant dates.

Quotation panels provide contemporary accounts of the events under discussion.

All articles end with cross-references to related articles.

CONTENTS

ALEXANDER THE GREAT

AT THE AGE OF TWENTY, ALEXANDER (356–323 BCE) was proclaimed king of Macedonia, a mountainous kingdom to the north of Greece. Perhaps the most accomplished general of all time, in thirteen years Alexander marched his army east and explored and conquered a considerable portion of the known world. For his remarkable enlargement of the Macedonian Empire, which, when he died, stretched some three thousand miles (4,828 km), from Greece to India, he later became known as Alexander the Great.

Below **This marble bust of Alexander is attributed to Lysippos, an influential Greek sculptor who flourished between 370 and 310 BCE.**

BORN TO BE KING
At age twelve Alexander is said to have tamed a wild stallion, which he named Bucephalus (meaning "ox head"). Realizing the horse was afraid of its own shadow, Alexander turned Bucephalus to face the sun. With its shadow behind it, the horse was calmed, and Alexander was able to mount it.

When Alexander was thirteen, his father, King Philip II, brought Aristotle (384–322 BCE), the leading Greek philosopher, to the Macedonian court. For three years Aristotle taught Alexander history, politics, and poetry and nurtured Alexander's interest in geography.

MACEDONIA'S RISE TO POWER
Philip had assembled a large army, and under his rule Macedonia became a powerful state. In 340 BCE he made Alexander his military deputy. In 338, aged eighteen, Alexander led the Macedonian cavalry at the Battle of Chaeronea, where his defeat of the Greeks gave Philip control of Greece. Philip next planned to free Greek cities in Asia Minor (present-day Turkey) from the rule of Persia, Greece's long-standing enemy. However, in 336, before he could begin his campaign, Philip was murdered.

ALEXANDER'S ARMY
Alexander—newly crowned King Alexander III of Macedonia—was determined to continue and add to his father's legacy. Intending to conquer the Persian Empire, which stretched from the Mediterranean shores to the banks of the Indus River, in spring 334 BCE he crossed the Hellespont, the narrow strait separating Europe from Asia.

Alexander's army of 43,000 foot soldiers and 5,500 cavalry was accompanied by geog-

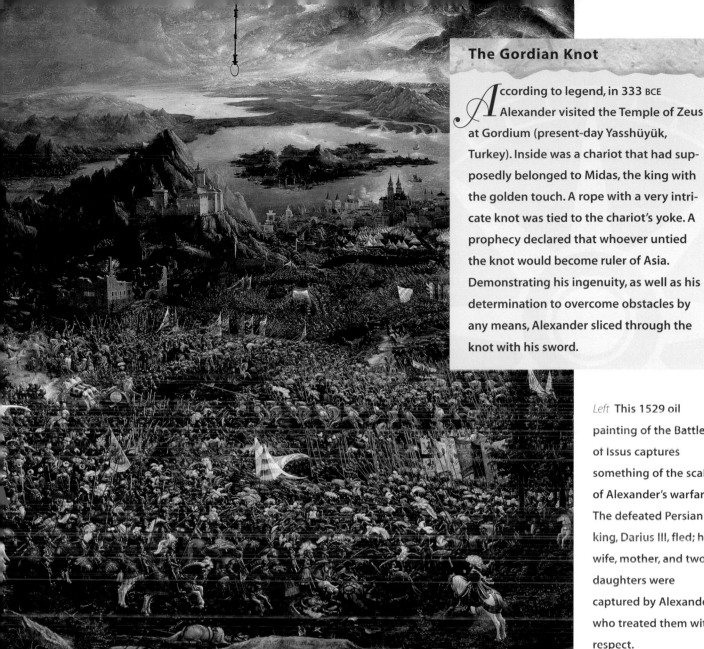

Left This 1529 oil painting of the Battle of Issus captures something of the scale of Alexander's warfare. The defeated Persian king, Darius III, fled; his wife, mother, and two daughters were captured by Alexander, who treated them with respect.

raphers, astronomers, mathematicians, botanists, and engineers. Their task was to collect information about the lands Alexander passed through as he crossed Asia. Specially trained runners (known as *bematistae*) who paced out the length of each day's march assisted the geographers in compiling their records and possibly in drafting maps.

ALEXANDER DEFEATS THE PERSIANS

Shortly after entering Asia Minor, Alexander's army won the Battle of the Granicus River (334 BCE) and began liberating the Greek cities from Persian control. The following year Alexander met the army of the Persian king Darius III at the Battle of Issus, in present-day southern Turkey. Though outnumbered two to one, Alexander inflicted a humiliating defeat on the Persians.

From Asia Minor, Alexander marched south through present-day Lebanon, captured the city of Tyre after an eight-month siege, crossed Palestine, and entered Egypt. The Egyptians welcomed him as their liberator from the Persians and declared him pharaoh (king) of Egypt. In 331 BCE he founded a city at the mouth of the Nile River, named Alexandria in his honor. This city was the first of about seventy Alexander founded, including around thirty named Alexandria.

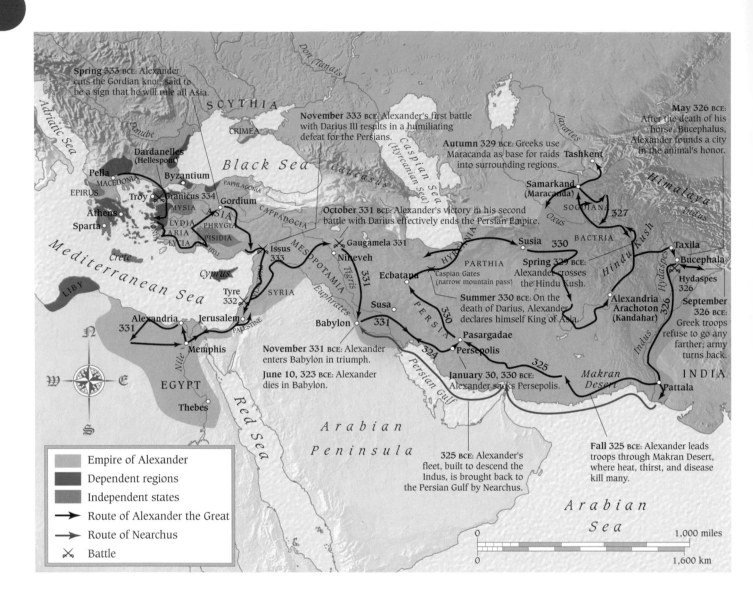

Spring 333 BCE: Alexander cuts the Gordian knot, said to be a sign that he will rule all Asia.

November 333 BCE: Alexander's first battle with Darius III results in a humiliating defeat for the Persians.

Autumn 329 BCE: Greeks use Maracanda as base for raids into surrounding regions.

May 326 BCE: After the death of his horse, Bucephalus, Alexander founds a city in the animal's honor.

October 331 BCE: Alexander's victory in his second battle with Darius effectively ends the Persian Empire.

Spring 329 BCE: Alexander crosses the Hindu Kush.

Summer 330 BCE: On the death of Darius, Alexander declares himself King of Asia.

November 331 BCE: Alexander enters Babylon in triumph.

June 10, 323 BCE: Alexander dies in Babylon.

January 30, 330 BCE: Alexander sacks Persepolis.

September 326 BCE: Greek troops refuse to go any farther; army turns back.

Fall 325 BCE: Alexander leads troops through Makran Desert, where heat, thirst, and disease kill many.

325 BCE: Alexander's fleet, built to descend the Indus, is brought back to the Persian Gulf by Nearchus.

Map legend:
- Empire of Alexander
- Dependent regions
- Independent states
- → Route of Alexander the Great
- → Route of Nearchus
- ✗ Battle

0 — 1,000 miles
0 — 1,600 km

Above **In the aftermath of Alexander's conquests, cities thousands of miles from Greece perpetuated the ideals of Greek civilization.**

Late in the year 331 BCE Alexander entered Mesopotamia and defeated the Persians at the Battle of Gaugamela (near present-day Erbil, Iraq). He went on to take control of the cities of Babylon, Persepolis, and Ecbatana and, on the death of Darius in 330, declared himself king of Asia.

ALEXANDER REACHES THE INDUS RIVER
Continuing eastward into lands then unknown to the Greeks, Alexander crossed the Hindu Kush Mountains and pursued enemy forces into central Asia. In 327 BCE he turned south to India. In several battles, notably the Battle of the Hydaspes River (326),

---

356 BCE
Alexander is born at Pella, Macedonia.

336
Becomes king of Macedonia.

334
Crosses the Hellespont into Asia Minor (Turkey).

332
Captures Tyre; arrives in Egypt and is crowned pharaoh.

331
Reaches the Tigris and Euphrates Rivers in Mesopotamia.

330
On the death of Darius III, declares himself king of Asia.

329–327
Marches through central Asia; crosses the Hindu Kush in present-day Afghanistan.

327–325
Turns south toward India and reaches the Indus River; establishes that the Indus and the Nile are not linked.

325
Divides his army in two and leads one half homeward overland.

323
Dies in Babylon and is buried in Alexandria, Egypt.

The Greek historian Arrian (c. 86–160 CE) attributed the following speech to Alexander:

. . . through your courage and endurance you have gained possession of Ionia, the Hellespont, both Phrygias, Cappadocia, Paphlagonia, Lydia, Caria, Lycia, Pamphylia, Phoenicia, and Egypt; the Greek part of Libya is now yours, together with much of Arabia, lowland Syria, Mesopotamia, Babylon, and Susia; Persia and Media with all the territories either formerly controlled by them or not are in your hands; you have made yourselves masters of the lands beyond the Caspian Gates, beyond the Caucasus, beyond the Tanais, of Bactria, Hyrcania, and the Hyrcanian sea; we have driven the Scythians back into the desert; and Indus and Hydaspes, Acesines and Hydraotes flow now through country which is ours.

Arrian, *The Campaigns of Alexander*

Alexander's army encountered war elephants for the first time. When his beloved horse, Bucephalus, died, Alexander founded the city of Bucephala in the animal's honor.

Alexander wanted to press on to the Ganges River, but his troops—who had been on campaign for eight years—refused to advance farther east. Alexander agreed to return home but wanted to establish first whether the Indus and Nile Rivers were connected—if they were, he intended to return to the Mediterranean by this route. Following the Indus River south, he marched to the Indian Ocean coast, where he divided his army in two. One part, under the command of Nearchus (360–312 BCE), sailed west along the northern coast of the Arabian Sea and into the Persian Gulf and thereby established that those two bodies of water are connected. Alexander took the second division overland across the deserts of Makran and on to Babylon. Thousands perished on the way, including Alexander, who died of a fever (probably malaria) at Babylon in June 323. His body was embalmed and carried to Alexandria, Egypt, for burial.

ALEXANDER'S ACHIEVEMENT

Alexander's 20,000-mile (32,000 km) march created the largest empire of the ancient world and brought him into contact with cultures previously unknown to the Greeks. His scientists collected information that greatly increased Greek (and, subsequently, Roman) knowledge of Asia. His pioneering route through modern Iran opened up the Silk Road, for fifteen hundred years a major trade highway between China and Europe.

SEE ALSO

• Colonization and Conquest • Silk Road

Above **This image of Alexander riding Bucephalus forms part of the so-called Alexander Mosaic, which dates from the first century BCE and once decorated the floor of a villa in Pompeii, in southern Italy.**

AMUNDSEN, ROALD

BORN IN 1872, THE GREAT NORWEGIAN POLAR EXPLORER Roald Amundsen was the first seafarer to transit the Northwest Passage—a goal that had eluded explorers for centuries and cost many lives. In 1911 Amundsen led the first expedition to reach the South Pole, and in 1925 he was a member of the first party to reach the North Pole by air. He died in 1928 while attempting to rescue fellow explorers missing in the Arctic.

EARLY PREPARATION

Roald Amundsen was born into a family of shipbuilders and developed an early fascination with polar exploration. He was determined to surpass the achievements of previous polar pioneers and left school at fifteen to go to sea. Aware of the rigors of polar exploration, he began early to prepare himself. Even in the depth of winter, he would sleep with the window open. He kept himself fit with a range of athletic activities, especially skiing.

Below **Roald Amundsen studies a map in the cabin of the *Gjøa*.**

FIRST EXPEDITION

In 1897 Amundsen was second mate aboard the *Belgica* on a voyage to Antarctica. The boat became trapped in ice, and the crew had to endure a pitiless winter with months of total darkness. Amundsen distinguished himself by his courage and readiness to face any emergency. The *Belgica* managed to escape the Antarctic ice but not before many of the crew had succumbed to scurvy and even to insanity.

The *Belgica* expedition gave Amundsen confidence that he could cope with any obstacles the polar regions might present him. In 1903 he and a crew of six set sail for Canada aboard the seventy-two-foot (22 m) boat *Gjøa*. He intended to complete a voyage

JULY 16, 1872
Roald Amundsen is born near Oslo.

1894
Works on an Arctic sealing ship.

1897–1899
Endures his first Antarctic winter aboard the *Belgica*.

1903–1906
Leads the first voyage to complete the Northwest Passage.

DECEMBER 14, 1911
Becomes the first explorer to reach the South Pole.

1918–1920
Sails through the Northeast Passage.

1926
Reaches the North Pole, along with Lincoln Ellsworth, Umberto Nobile, and the crew of the airship *Norge*.

JUNE 1928
Dies in the Arctic while searching for survivors of the airship *Italia*.

through the Northwest Passage, a fiendishly complex route through an intricate network of icy passages in the Canadian Arctic. Sailing from east to west, in 1906 the *Gjøa* became the first vessel to complete the entire journey.

LOOKING NORTH

Amundsen's success helped him secure financial backing for his next venture, a journey to the North Pole. A fellow Norwegian, Fridtjof Nansen, who had narrowly failed to reach the Pole in 1895, lent Amundsen his research vessel, the *Fram*.

Just as Amundsen was set to depart, it was announced that the American explorer Robert E. Peary had beaten him to the North Pole. Amundsen abandoned his plans in an instant and decided to set sail for the South Pole instead. He did not tell his backers, for he

At the South Pole, Amundsen commented on the perpetual daylight of polar summer:

It was very strange to turn in at 6 PM, and then on turning out again at midnight to find the sun apparently still at the same altitude, and then once more at 6 AM to see it still no higher.

Roald Amundsen, *The South Pole*

Above **This 1900 engraving of the** *Belgica's* **winter in the Antarctic depicts the crew burying Lieutenant Dance, who died from a heart attack.**

was deeply in debt and knew that some of them would not support such an apparently foolhardy expedition. He also knew that a British expedition under Robert Falcon Scott was about to depart for the South Pole. Reaching the Pole first would bring Amundsen lasting fame and, just as important, funds for further expeditions.

Above **On December 14, 1911, Amundsen was photographed at the South Pole, flying the Norwegian flag and surrounded by the dogs who had taken him there.**

THE SOUTH POLE TREK

When the *Fram* set sail in June 1910, nobody but Amundsen and his brother knew of the change of plans. In January 1911 the ship, loaded with ninety-seven Greenland dogs, a crew of just nineteen men, and wood for a large hut, reached the Bay of Whales, where Amundsen's men set up a base. Before winter set in, the team laid down a series of food depots on the way to the Pole. They also constructed comfortable quarters in which to spend the coming months.

Amundsen's concern that Scott would beat him to the Pole led him to make the one great error of his expedition. When spring arrived in late August 1911, he set off too early. The weather turned brutal, and his men made a hasty retreat, lucky to escape with only minor frostbite. Amundsen and four other men set off again on October 19, together with fifty-two dogs and four sleds.

The weather remained favorable as the men edged toward the Pole, traveling perhaps twenty miles a day. Their steady progress was due in no small measure to good planning and pragmatic use of dogs. As supplies were used up, dogs were shot and their carcasses fed to the remaining dogs.

Amundsen and his team reached the South Pole in good health on December 14, 1911. They celebrated with seal meat and cigars, made observations to confirm their location, and then returned. Scott reached the Pole over a month later, his team's sleds having been man-hauled. He and his four companions all died on the return journey.

FAME BUT NOT FORTUNE

In a new ship, the *Maud*, Amundsen led further expeditions, including a renewed attempt to get to the North Pole and a voyage through the Northeast Passage (1918–1920). By 1924 Amundsen was in desperate need of money and was delighted to team up with the wealthy American explorer Lincoln Ellsworth. In 1926, aboard the airship *Norge,* the two men, together with the Italian airship designer Umberto Nobile and a small crew, became the first people to fly to 90° N— the top of the world.

However, Amundsen's association with Nobile was to lead to the Norwegian's demise. In 1928 Nobile set out for the North Pole in another airship, the *Italia,* which crashed. Ships and planes set out to rescue the survivors (Nobile and seven companions were eventually found alive). Among those attempting the rescue was Amundsen, who borrowed a French seaplane for the purpose. Overloaded and unsuited to Arctic conditions, the plane was lost at sea, and Amundsen was never seen again.

A WINTER EVENING AT FRAMHEIM.

Amundsen's Team

While Robert Falcon Scott and his team became household names, Amundsen's fellow travelers were soon forgotten. With Amundsen at the South Pole were Olav Bjaarland, Helmer Hanssen, Sverre Hassel, and Oskar Wisting. Each made an important contribution, especially Bjaarland, who was an exceptional skier, and Hanssen, who was a gifted dog handler. Hassel died in 1928 during a visit to his former leader (he in fact dropped dead at Amundsen's feet). Wisting's death was even stranger. In 1936 he returned to visit the *Fram* and asked to spend the night in his old cabin. He was found dead in the morning.

Above These photographs, from Amundsen's own account of his South Pole expedition, depict daily life at the Norwegians' base in Antarctica during the winter of 1911. The men named their base Framheim (*Fram*'s home).

SEE ALSO

ANTHROPOLOGY

ANTHROPOLOGY IS THE SCIENCE OF HUMAN BEINGS; the word derives from *anthropos*, the Greek word for "human being." Cultural anthropologists, also known as ethnologists, study the social arrangements of different peoples, especially family structures, languages, technologies, and belief systems. Physical anthropology is concerned mainly with the evolution of biological human characteristics; practitioners often study humans in relation to their primate ancestors. Since the origin of the science of anthropology, explorers have supplied anthropologists with a great deal of valuable data, gathered during encounters with peoples living in remote or inaccessible areas.

Below **This staged photograph of an Indonesian princess standing against a painted backcloth is typical of the pictures taken by nineteenth-century anthropologists.**

EARLY ROOTS

The roots of anthropology lie in the writings of travelers in the ancient world, who recorded the way foreign peoples lived and behaved and what they believed in. The Greek writer Herodotus of Halicarnassus (c. 490–425 BCE), for example, traveled widely in western Asia and described peoples such as the Persians and the Scythians. Although generally thought of as a historian (his monumental work of 440 BCE is called *Histories*), Herodotus had an anthropologist's interest in the practices of different peoples, such as Egyptian mummification of the dead.

A similar passion for anthropology can be found in the writings of medieval travelers. The Venetian Marco Polo (1254–1324) described the customs of the inhabitants of China and central Asia. In 1431 another

c. 440 BCE
Herodotus completes the *Histories*.

1298 CE
Marco Polo describes his encounters with peoples of Asia.

1432
Pietro Querini, a shipwrecked Venetian, describes the Lofoten islanders' way of life.

1869
The American Museum and Library of Natural History is founded in New York.

1874
The invention of the dry-plate glass negative allows explorers to take photographs of other peoples.

The Camera

During the second half of the nineteenth century, the science of photography developed to the extent that travelers were able to carry photographic equipment. Photographs of native peoples were thought by most anthropologists to constitute unbiased and objective scientific evidence (as opposed to the sketches that earlier explorers had provided).

From 1860 leading anthropological museums began to amass huge collections of ethnographic photographs. However, some modern anthropologists believe that many of these early photographs are not as objective as was once thought. It is argued that nineteenth-century anthropologists deliberately selected images that accorded with their view of indigenous peoples as primitive or barbaric. Such anthropologists allegedly overlooked situations that proved native peoples had adopted some more advanced habits and behaviors.

Some indigenous peoples fear the camera, believing that by taking a photograph a person steals the subject's soul. In the 1890s the African Gaza chief Gungunhana refused to be photographed by visitors to his capital, Mandlakazi (in present-day southern Mozambique). Gunqunhana feared that the camera would take away his royal power.

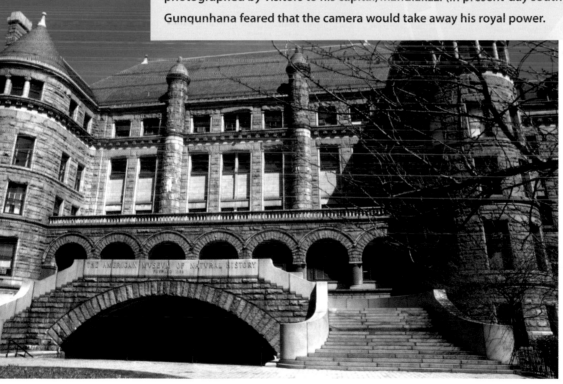

Left **The anthropological collections of the American Museum of Natural History in New York reveal much about the culture of the native peoples of the Americas and Oceania.**

1884
The Pitt Rivers Museum is founded in Oxford, England.

1911
Franz Boas publishes *The Mind of Primitive Man*.

1928
Margaret Mead publishes *Coming of Age in Samoa*.

1999
Scotland's Glasgow Kelvingrove Museum returns the Lakota ghost shirt to the Sioux.

Venetian, Pietro Querini, was blown by a storm to the Lofoten Islands, off northern Norway. Coming from the richest and most sophisticated city in Europe, Querini was impressed by the simple virtue of the Lofoten islanders' way of life. He noted their honesty and trustworthiness, as well as their custom of using dried fish as money. Querini's account stands as a fine example of anthropological writing before the era of modern science.

THE FATHER OF AMERICAN ANTHROPOLOGY

Anthropology became a widely recognized science in the second half of the nineteenth century. Among the most influential practitioners during this period was Franz Boas (1858–1942), often called the father of American anthropology. Born in Minden, Germany, Boas became a professor at Columbia University in 1899.

While working among the native peoples of British Columbia, Boas made an important discovery. He found it difficult to record the sounds of the Kwakiutl language (and of several other languages spoken by Indian peoples native to the Vancouver area). For example, he recorded the native Tlingit word for fear as both "baec" and "pas." Earlier researchers had written off such variations as a sign of the primitiveness of the Indian languages. Boas, on the other hand, was the first anthropologist to realize that the problem lay in his own unfamiliarity with non-European language sounds. This realization led Boas to develop his theory of cultural relativism. According to this theory, all human cultures are complex and highly developed. Peoples are different because they have developed in ways that have been shaped by their particular social and environmental conditions. One culture is not inherently superior to another: cultures are simply different.

Boas's ideas ran counter to the general belief of nineteenth-century anthropologists that non-European cultures in Asia, Africa, and the Americas were at an earlier stage of evolution.

COLLECTORS AND MUSEUMS

Explorers played an important role in the development of anthropology in Europe and North America. Many nineteenth-century explorers collected unfamiliar objects and recorded their impressions of indigenous peoples. Many of these explorers later donated their collections to museums, or even founded museums to house their collections. For example, the founding of the American Museum and Library of Natural History in New York in 1869 resulted from the nineteenth-century appetite for collecting and classifying so-called scientific curiosities from around the world. The Pitt Rivers Museum was founded in Oxford, England, in 1884, when the British explorer Lt. General Pitt Rivers gave his collection of eighteen thousand artifacts, gathered from native peoples around the world, to Oxford University.

Below **Franz Boas, the subject of this 1906 photograph, used new technologies, such as the movie camera and sound recording, in his fieldwork.**

Margaret Mead *1901–1978*

$\mathcal{T}$he work of Franz Boas had a profound influence on Margaret Mead, perhaps the best-known American anthropologist of the twentieth century. Mead worked at the American Museum of Natural History in New York from 1926 until her death and did more than any other anthropologist to explain her subject to the general public.

As a young woman Mead traveled to the South Pacific to study the way that children and teenagers grew up in American Samoa and New Guinea. Her 1928 book, *Coming of Age in Samoa*, was a best-seller around the world. In it she put forward for the first time the argument that the way children and teenagers grow up is heavily influenced by the values and expectations of the adults around them. Mead believed that Samoan teenagers were happier and more relaxed than American teenagers because Samoan adults were more sympathetic and understanding of the problems that adolescents experience.

Mead's interests went far beyond anthropology. She proposed that if American teenagers were treated differently by school and family, they would experience fewer social and personal problems. Since the 1980s other scholars have scrutinized and questioned Mead's research methods and conclusions, but her influence remains substantial.

Below Mead visited the Manus people of Papua New Guinea in 1929 and again in 1953. On her second trip she noted how Manus life had been changed by contact with the West.

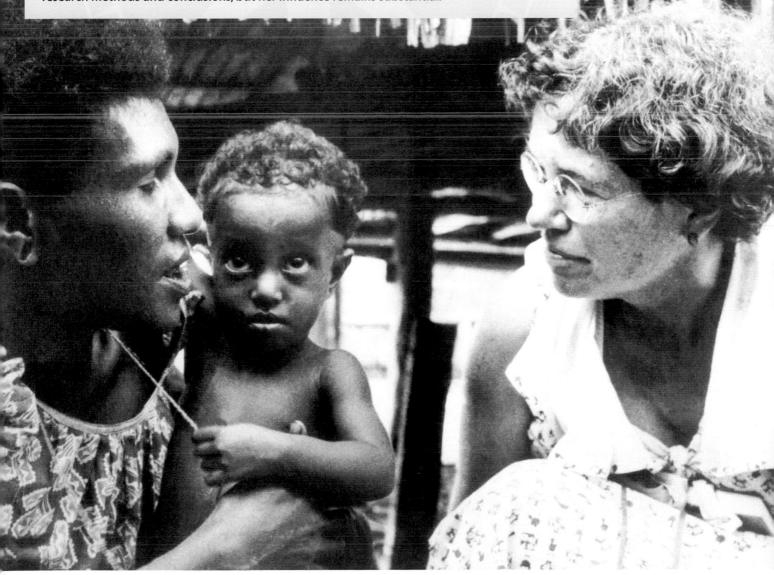

Above **Several American Indian peoples believed that ghost shirts offered magical protection from attacks. Such objects were highly prized by anthropologists, and many were seized.**

Margaret Mead made the point that anthropology helps Western society to understand its own way of life, not just that of the peoples being studied:

As the traveler who has once been from home is wiser than he who has never left his own doorstep, so a knowledge of one other culture should sharpen our ability to scrutinize more steadily, to appreciate more lovingly, our own.

Margaret Mead, *Coming of Age in Samoa*

The Field Museum in Chicago had its origins in the World's Columbian Exposition, an international fair held in that city in 1893. The museum's vast collection, consisting of over twenty million objects, has grown through its funding of major anthropological projects, such as expeditions to Melanesia and the Philippines between 1908 and 1915, as well as bequests from significant collectors.

The practice of collecting items in one place in a museum was a major factor in the development of the science of anthropology in the nineteenth and twentieth centuries. Museums enabled scholars to analyze and compare similar artifacts, an important procedure in anthropological study. There was great competition among museums in Europe and North America for important or rare objects. This competition created an international market in artifacts originating from areas of the world where native cultures preserved traditional ways of life.

During the later part of the twentieth century, museums were criticized for owning items that had been taken, often by force, from native peoples. In many cases, museums agreed to return important items to their original owners. In 1999 the Glasgow Kelvingrove Museum, in Scotland, returned the famous Lakota ghost shirt, which it had acquired after the 1890 massacre of Lakota Sioux Indians by U.S. cavalrymen at Wounded Knee, South Dakota. In the twenty-first century, anthropological museums tend to be wary of displaying such sensitive material as sacred objects and human remains.

SEE ALSO
- Museums • Native Peoples • Photography
- Record Keeping

ARMSTRONG, NEIL

NEIL ALDEN ARMSTRONG ACHIEVED one of the greatest single feats in the history of exploration on July 20, 1969, when he became the first person in history to walk on the surface of the moon. Although his name alone will forever be associated with that achievement, he was only one part of a well-funded team of NASA experts that made his journey to the moon possible.

AIMING HIGH

Born in Wapakoneta, Ohio, in 1930, Neil Armstrong qualified as a pilot when he was just sixteen. He studied aeronautical engineering at Purdue University, in Indiana, and entered the military as a naval aviator. During the 1950s Armstrong's service in the Korean War earned him three medals for bravery.

In 1955 he began work as a research pilot for the National Advisory Committee for Aeronautics (NACA). In 1958 that organization was replaced by the National Aeronautics and Space Administration (NASA). During the next few years Armstrong piloted test flights of jets, helicopters, early supersonic planes, and rockets.

DOCKING IN SPACE

In 1962 Armstrong joined NASA's space program and was selected to become a member of the Project Gemini team. After acting as a backup astronaut for several space flights, in 1966 Armstrong was given the chance to fly into space himself. On March 16 he and David R. Scott were launched from the Kennedy Space Center at Cape Canaveral, Florida, in *Gemini 8*. As commander of the flight, Armstrong's mission was to engineer a linkup with an unmanned rocket—the first-ever docking in space. However, after the docking maneuver, *Gemini 8* developed a serious fault. Although Armstrong's quick actions enabled the spacecraft to be stabilized, the mission was aborted, and *Gemini 8* made an emergency splashdown in the Pacific Ocean.

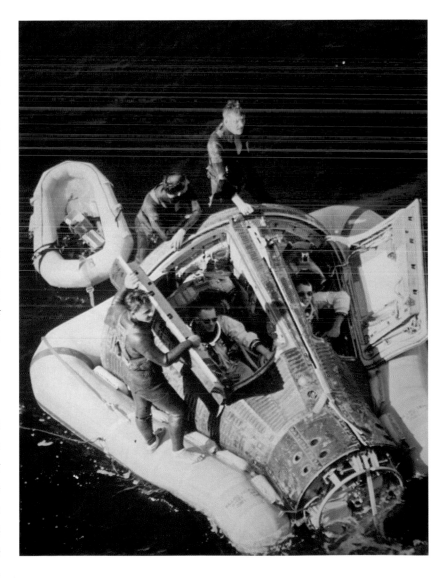

Above **A rescue team reaches *Gemini 8* after its emergency splashdown in 1966.**

LIFTOFF

In 1961 President John F. Kennedy had declared that the United States would send an American astronaut to the moon before the end of the decade. NASA launched Project Apollo to realize Kennedy's vision.

Below **Neil Armstrong rehearses the launch of** *Apollo 11.*

After the first Apollo flights had made observations of the moon during lunar orbits, NASA announced that *Apollo 11*, commanded by Armstrong, would be the first manned spacecraft to land on the moon's surface.

On the morning of July 16, 1969, a global radio and television audience of hundreds of thousands witnessed Neil Armstrong, Edwin E. Aldrin Jr. (nicknamed Buzz), and Michael Collins stepping aboard *Apollo 11*. At 9:37 AM they lifted off from the Kennedy Space Center.

THE *EAGLE* LANDS

Armstrong and Aldrin were to take the lunar landing module, named *Eagle*, down to the surface while Collins remained in charge of the command module. On July 20, 1969, four days after takeoff, the two modules separated, and Armstrong and Aldrin began their descent toward the moon. Although clouds of dust blocked the astronauts' view as they were about to touch down, Armstrong and Aldrin managed to land the *Eagle* safely near the Sea of Tranquillity. At 10:56 PM (EDT), Armstrong became the first person in history to step onto the moon. Aldrin followed him nineteen minutes later.

During the next couple of hours, Armstrong and Aldrin explored the area around the *Eagle*. They took photos and film footage, gathered rock samples, planted the U.S. flag, and laid a plaque that read "Here men from the planet Earth first set foot upon the moon, July 1969 AD. We came in peace for all mankind."

AUGUST 5, 1930
Neil Armstrong is born.

1949
Becomes a U.S. Navy pilot.

1955
Becomes a research pilot for NACA (later NASA).

1962
Joins NASA space program.

1966
Performs the first manned space docking, in *Gemini 8*.

JULY 16, 1969
Lifts off in *Apollo 11*.

JULY 20, 1969
Walks on the moon.

JULY 24, 1969
Splashes down in the Pacific Ocean.

1971
Resigns from NASA.

On July 20, 1969, the first words of Neil Armstrong as he stepped down the *Eagle's* ladder and set foot on the moon were heard by millions of people around the world:

That's one small step for [a] man; one giant leap for mankind . . . the surface is fine and powdery. I can kick it up loosely with my toe. It does adhere in fine layers, like powdered charcoal, to the sole and sides of my boots. . . . There seems to be no difficulty in moving around, as we suspected. . . . It's absolutely no trouble to walk around. . . . It has a stark beauty all its own. It's like much of the high desert of the United States. It's different, but it's very pretty out here.

BACK DOWN TO EARTH

The docking between the lunar-landing module and the command module was successful, and Armstrong, Aldrin, and Collins returned to earth safely. On July 24, *Apollo 11* splashed down in the Pacific Ocean.

Armstrong was responsible for aeronautics research and technology at NASA until 1971, when he left the organization to become professor of aerospace engineering at the University of Cincinnati in Ohio and to run his own computer company. In 1986 he was part of the team that investigated the *Challenger* space shuttle disaster, in which seven astronauts were lost shortly after takeoff.

SEE ALSO

- Astronauts • Glenn, John • NASA
- Shepard, Alan B., Jr. • Spacecraft
- Space Exploration

Above **Neil Armstrong will always be remembered as the person who left the first human footprint on the moon.**

ASHLEY, WILLIAM HENRY

IN THE EARLY 1820S, AFTER A YOUTH spent in mining, the militia, and politics, William Henry Ashley started a business that brought scores of adventurous men into the Rocky Mountain fur trade. Ashley's mountain men, as they became known, pioneered the exploration of areas of the Rocky Mountain region. After leaving the fur business, Ashley again devoted his energies to politics (with some success) until his death in 1838.

Right **Saint Louis was already a bustling center for the fur trade when William Ashley placed this ad in the** *Missouri Gazette.*

TO
Enterprising Young Men.

THE subscriber wishes to engage ONE HUNDRED MEN, to ascend the river Missouri to its source, there to be employed for one, two or three years.—For particulars, enquire of Major Andrew Henry, near the Lead Mines, in the County of Washington, (who will ascend with, and command the party) or to the subscriber at St. Louis.

Wm. H. Ashley.

February 13 ———98 tf

TO THE WEST

William Ashley moved to Missouri in his mid-twenties. He started out mining saltpeter, an ingredient of gunpowder, and later joined with Andrew Henry to mine lead. The partners moved into manufacturing gunpowder, a commodity whose value was greatly boosted during the War of 1812, fought between the Americans and the British. Ashley became first a general in Missouri's militia and then that state's first lieutenant governor.

THE MOUNTAIN MEN

After the war Henry suggested to Ashley that they enter into a new business venture together. Years before, Henry had been involved in the fur trade along the Missouri River. He convinced Ashley that the fur business could yield great profits but argued that

| **1778** William Henry Ashley is born in Virginia. | **1820** Is elected lieutenant governor of Missouri. | **1824** Henry leaves the partnership. | **1826** Retires from fur business. | **1836** Loses election for governor of Missouri. |
| **c. 1804** Moves to Missouri. | **1822** Launches fur business with Andrew Henry. | **1825** Ashley explores Green River; holds first rendezvous. | **1831** Wins election to Congress. | **1838** Dies in Missouri. |

the traditional approach, which relied on Native Americans collecting the furs, should be overhauled. He proposed recruiting men to go into the mountains and get the furs themselves.

Eager to make his fortune, Ashley agreed. On February 13, 1822, he ran an advertisement in the *Missouri Gazette*, asking for "one hundred men, to ascend the river Missouri to its source, there to be employed for one, two or three years." The notice attracted considerable attention. Jim Bridger and Jedediah Strong Smith were among the men who joined Ashley's team of mountain men.

In 1849 a British writer described the mountain men:

Strong, active, hardy as bears, daring, expert in the use of their weapons, they are just what uncivilized white man might be supposed to be in a brute state, depending upon his instinct for the support of life. . . . From the Mississippi to the mouth of the Colorado of the West, from the frozen regions of the North to the Gila in Mexico, the beaver-hunter has set his traps in every creek and stream. All this vast country, but for the daring enterprise of these men, would be even now a terra incognita to geographers; . . . but there is not an acre that has not been passed and repassed by the trappers in their perilous excursions.

George F. Ruxton, *Adventures in Mexico and the Rocky Mountains*

EXPLORING THE WEST

Attempts to set up a fur-trapping enterprise on the upper Missouri were unsuccessful. It proved difficult to get supplies to the far-flung trappers, and Native Americans in the region were hostile. In 1823 a large force of Arikara Indians attacked a group of trappers and killed many of Ashley's men.

In 1824, when Henry pulled out of the business, Ashley decided to move the trappers into the mountains south of the Missouri River. He also had the idea of gathering the

Below **A mountain man plants a beaver trap in one of the streams that flow through the Rocky Mountains.**

Above **Jim Beckwourth (1798–c. 1867), a frontiersman whose life was full of adventure, became one of Ashley's mountain men in 1824 and attended the first rendezvous at Henry's Fork, on the Green River.**

men at the end of the trapping season in one spot, where they could turn over their furs and receive fresh supplies for the next season's hunt. Such a gathering is known as a rendezvous.

The first rendezvous was held in 1825 in the Green River valley, in present-day southern Wyoming. To meet the trappers, Ashley had to travel from a fort in eastern Nebraska over the front ranges of the Rockies in the dead of winter. It was a long and difficult journey, made worthwhile by the excellent haul of furs he brought in.

The 1826 rendezvous also produced a rich haul of furs. After selling that year's stock, Ashley sold his company to Jedediah Strong Smith and two colleagues. From that point forward, Ashley simply sold supplies to their company.

A POLITICAL CAREER

Ashley spent the rest of his life in politics. Having already run for governor of Missouri in 1824—and lost—in 1829 he lost a campaign for the U.S. Senate. Two years later, he was elected to the first of three terms in the House of Representatives. In 1836 he lost the governorship once again. Two years later Ashley died.

SEE ALSO

- Astor, John Jacob • Bridger, Jim • Carson, Kit
- Smith, Jedediah Strong

Astor, John Jacob

A CLASSIC RAGS-TO-RICHES TALE, the life of John Jacob Astor began in poverty in 1763 and ended in fabulous wealth in 1848. Astor came to the newly formed United States with little money. Through hard work, a frugal nature, a willingness to exercise power, and the help of his wife, Astor accumulated an immense fortune, partly from profits from the fur trade. As one of the earliest businessmen to engage in the fur trade in the Pacific Northwest, he sponsored explorations of the region from Washington state to the Rocky Mountains.

LIFE IN EUROPE

John Jacob Astor was born in Germany in 1763 to a family that struggled to get by. Astor's father's career as a butcher was unsuccessful. Two of Astor's older brothers left home, one for Britain and one for the United States. When his mother died and his father made plans to remarry, the seventeen-year-old John Jacob also left home. He planned to join his brother George in London but did not have the money to pay for the passage. Nevertheless, he managed to work his way to Britain and finally landed in London.

George Astor made musical instruments, and John Jacob worked for him for three years. During this period, John Jacob was waiting until it became possible to travel to America, which was then fighting a war for independence from Britain.

In 1783 Britain signed the Treaty of Paris, an official recognition of the independence of the United States of America. Astor lost little time, and by November he was on a ship bound for the new country. He left with twenty-five dollars, seven flutes, and a good deal of ambition and determination.

Right **Astor was called "one of the ablest, boldest, and most successful operators that ever lived" and also "a self-invented money-making machine."**

RISING IN BUSINESS

During the voyage to America, Astor met a fellow German who had traded with Indians for furs—Astor may have learned much from their discussion. Having settled in New York, Astor spent a few years in different businesses. Although he improved his financial position, he gained no great wealth. In 1786 he married Sarah Todd, who knew how to judge the quality of furs, and soon after, Astor moved into the fur business. By buying furs in Canada and selling them in Britain, he slowly amassed a fortune. He won the right to sell his goods in some ports of China, an arrangement that greatly extended his reach. Meanwhile, he began to buy property in the growing city of New York.

PLANNING AN EMPIRE

In 1803 the United States purchased the vast Louisiana Territory from France, an act that opened the way to the Rocky Mountains and the Pacific Northwest. Astor wanted to open a trading post on the Pacific coast, where he planned to gather furs to be shipped to China. In China his ships would be able to pick up Chinese goods to sell in Europe. In Europe goods would be bought to sell in America.

In 1810 Astor and four partners formed the Pacific Fur Company. The next year, a ship sent by the company landed at the mouth of the Columbia River (on the border of present-day Washington and Oregon). Astor's men built a

1763
John Jacob Astor is born in Germany.

1780
Leaves home to join his brother in London.

1783
Leaves London for the United States.

1786
Opens his own business in New York City; marries.

1808
Forms the American Fur Company.

1810
Forms the Pacific Fur Company.

1811
Fort Astoria is built.

1813
Fort Astoria is sold.

1816
A federal law excludes foreign-owned companies from the fur trade.

1834
Astor sells his fur businesses.

1848
Dies.

In an 1836 account of Astor's fur business, the American writer Washington Irving described Astor's character:

He began his career, of course, on the narrowest scale; but he brought to the task a persevering industry, rigid economy, and strict integrity. To these were added an aspiring spirit that always looked upwards; a genius bold, fertile, and expansive; a sagacity quick to grasp and convert every circumstance to its advantage, and a singular and never wavering confidence of signal success.

Washington Irving, *Astoria, or, Anecdotes of an enterprise beyond the Rocky Mountains*

accepting competition. (At the time, both the United States and Britain claimed Oregon.) In 1812 Britain and the United States again went to war, and Astor's men were forced to sell the fort to the North West Company and leave.

EXPLORING THE WEST

A few of Astor's men decided to retrace their march back to the United States overland. The arduous journey, which took nearly a year, followed much of the route that later became the Oregon Trail. The men, led by Robert Stuart, endured great hardships. At one point, facing starvation, one of the party suggested they draw lots to see who should die so that the others could eat him. Stuart refused to allow this gruesome course of action, though, and soon after, the party found food. The men discovered the South Pass, a twenty-mile passage through the Rocky Mountains that was wide enough to accommodate wagons. Astor kept knowledge of this route to himself. Only when Jedediah Strong Smith found South Pass in 1824 did its existence become publicly known.

Above **In his painting *The Oregon Trail,* Albert Bierstadt depicted settlers heading to the Pacific Northwest along the route pioneered by fur traders.**

fort, which they named Fort Astoria. A second group, sent overland from Montreal, arrived at Fort Astoria in early 1812.

The fort did not last long, however. Astor's small band of traders was threatened by agents of the North West Company, a British firm that had long dominated the fur business in the region and had no intention of

GAINING POWER

Still determined to gain control of the fur trade, Astor tried an overland approach instead. He persuaded Congress to outlaw foreign-owned companies from the fur trade, and in so doing, he knocked out the North West Company.

LATER YEARS

Further competition came from Saint Louis–based American-owned companies. Astor sent trappers into the Rocky Mountains, but the Saint Louis trappers were more experienced and got better results. Astor's company never achieved the rousing success he had hoped for, and by 1834 he had tired of the fur business and sold out.

During the remainder of his life, Astor increased his real estate empire and became by far the wealthiest man in America. When he died in 1848, his estate was valued at twenty million dollars.

Below **New York's Waldorf-Astoria Hotel was originally built on the site later occupied by the Empire State Building. When that skyscraper was built, a new hotel, depicted here, was erected farther uptown in 1931.**

SEE ALSO
- Ashley, William Henry
- Smith, Jedediah Strong

ASTRONAUTS

ASTRONAUTS ARE EXPLORERS OF SPACE. The word *astronaut* comes from two Greek words that together mean "star sailor." In the short time from 1961, when the first person traveled into space, to the end of the twentieth century, several prominent astronauts and cosmonauts (the Russian equivalent) achieved remarkable feats at great risk to themselves. The advance in space travel technology has been rapid, and there is a real possibility that astronauts will travel to other planets before the end of the twenty-first century.

Below **Carrying the first person into space, *Vostok 1* is launched from the Baikonur cosmodrome in Kazakhstan, in Central Asia, in 1961.**

ROCKET SCIENCE

The basis of space travel is the rocket engine, which provides sufficient thrust to propel a vehicle beyond the earth's atmosphere and, as it carries its own oxygen, works in space. The first theoretical studies of rocket-propulsion systems were made by the Russian Konstantin Tsiolkovsky (1857–1935). In the first decades of the twentieth century, the American physicist Robert Goddard (1882–1945) designed the first successful liquid-fuel propulsion system, a technology that was used for the first manned rocket flights during the 1960s.

FIRST SPACE EXPLORERS

During the 1960s the Soviet Union and the United States competed in the so-called space race. In a sense, the competition was healthy, for each spurred the other on to ever greater achievements. On April 12, 1961, in *Vostok 1*, the Russian cosmonaut Yury Gagarin became the first person to travel into space and orbit the earth. Twenty-three days later, Alan B. Shepard Jr., the first U.S. astronaut in space, made a suborbital flight (that is, an incomplete orbit of the earth) aboard *Freedom 7*. In 1962 Shepard's colleague John Glenn surpassed Gagarin's achievement by traveling around the earth three times. In 1963 the Russian Valentina Tereshkova became the first female space traveler.

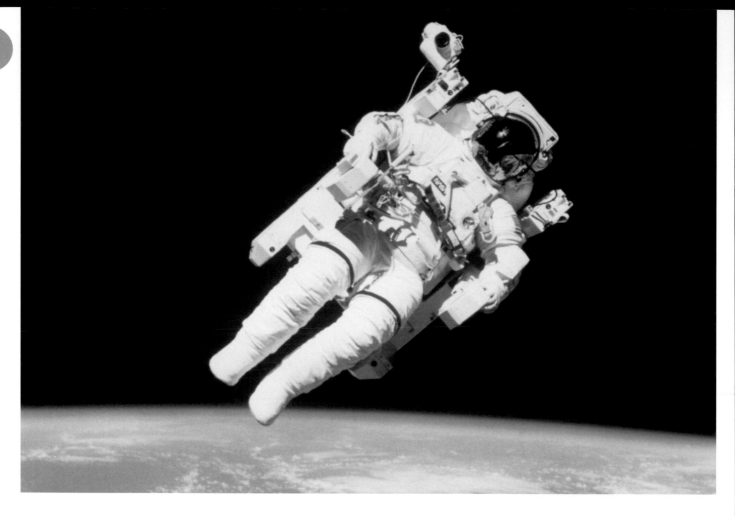

Above **In 1984 the U.S. astronaut Bruce McCandless, shown here, floated freely in space in the manned maneuvering unit (MMU) he helped design. Small nitrogen thrusters propel the first human satellite through space.**

WALKING IN SPACE

On March 18, 1965, the cosmonaut Alexei Leonov became the first person to climb out of a spacecraft in space. For twelve minutes, tethered to *Voskhod 2,* Leonov took pictures and practiced maneuvering in zero gravity. In June of the same year, the U.S. astronaut Edward White climbed out of *Gemini 4* and, during a twenty-minute space walk, moved about effortlessly with the help of a handheld maneuvering unit (HHMU), which somewhat resembled a rocket gun.

Space walks are now a relatively regular feature of space travel. While outside the spacecraft, astronauts wear reinforced suits to protect them from micrometeoroids, tiny floating pieces of rock, dust or space debris. An "umbilical cord" connected early space suits to the spacecraft. The cord exchanged oxygen for carbon dioxide, supplied cool air to prevent overheating, and allowed radio contact with those still on board. Later space suits were constructed with self-contained life-support systems, thanks to which the

1926
Robert Goddard carries out the first tests on liquid-propelled rockets.

APRIL 12, 1961
Yury Gagarin becomes the first person in space.

MAY 5, 1961
Alan B. Shepard Jr. takes part in the first manned American spaceflight.

FEBRUARY 20, 1962
John Glenn becomes the first U.S. astronaut to orbit the earth.

JUNE 16, 1963
Valentina Tereshkova becomes the first woman in space.

MARCH 18, 1965
Alexei Leonov makes the first space walk.

JUNE 3, 1965
Edward White makes the first U.S. space walk.

DECEMBER 1968
Apollo 8 is the first manned spacecraft to orbit the moon.

JANUARY 1969
Soyuz 4 and *Soyuz 5* stage the first transfer of astronauts in space.

JULY 20, 1969
Neil Armstrong and Buzz Aldrin become the first people to walk on the moon.

APRIL 19, 1971
Salyut 1 becomes the world's first manned space station.

MAY 14, 1973
Skylab, the first U.S. space station, is launched.

Edwin Eugene Aldrin Jr. BORN *1930*

$\mathcal{E}$dwin Aldrin, usually known by the nickname Buzz, began his astronaut training in 1963 and flew into space for the first time in 1966. During that flight, aboard *Gemini 12,* Aldrin's five-and-a-half-hour space walk proved that astronauts could survive and function for long periods of time in the vacuum of space.

Aldrin's next spaceflight, aboard *Apollo 11,* captured the attention of people all over the world. On July 20, 1969, Aldrin and Neil Armstrong landed on the moon and became the first people to walk on its surface. Although Armstrong took the first steps and received the greater part of the fame, Aldrin's achievements have ensured his own place in history.

astronauts were entirely free to propel themselves around.

DOCKING IN SPACE

On March 16, 1966, the astronaut Neil Armstrong, piloting *Gemini 8,* successfully performed the first docking maneuver (the linking of two craft) in space. Space stations are now constructed by docking separate units together high above the earth—a space station would be too large to send to space in one piece. Docking also allows spacecraft to transport astronauts between the earth and the International Space Station.

Right **On July 20, 1969, Buzz Aldrin stepped down from the lunar module and became the second person to walk on the moon.**

JULY 1975	FEBRUARY 1, 2003
The docking of *Soyuz 19* and *Apollo 18* is the first international space project.	After *Columbia* is destroyed on reentering the earth's atmosphere, the space shuttle program is indefinitely suspended.
APRIL 12, 1981	
The first space shuttle, *Columbia,* lifts off.	

LIVING IN SPACE

Yury Gagarin's first space flight in 1961 lasted just one hour, forty-eight minutes. In the decades that followed, progress in space technology enabled astronauts to live in space for months at a time. Research carried out by astronauts orbiting earth will prove invaluable if manned flights to other planets—which may take months or even years to complete—are launched.

DINNER IN A VACUUM

The first meals eaten in space were bland concoctions prepared as small cubes, freeze-dried powder, or a thick liquid in a tube. Astronauts' food improved dramatically during the last decades of the twentieth century, and at the beginning of the twenty-first century a typical evening meal on a space shuttle might have consisted of macaroni and cheese, fruit cocktail, and a strawberry drink.

Before a space flight, all food is carefully prepared and packaged to ensure that it stays edible for the duration of the mission. Any fresh food taken on board must be eaten at the beginning of a flight. It is much more difficult to eat and digest in the weightless conditions of space than it is on earth. Food must be easy to handle—for instance, it is vital that stray crumbs are not left floating around, as they could damage instrument panels or obstruct an astronaut's breathing equipment. To prevent drops of liquid from escaping, drinks are contained in bags and sucked through a straw. At the beginning of the twenty-first century, research was underway into the possibility of having astronauts grow their own cereals in space.

WORKING IN SPACE

During a space flight astronauts perform a variety of tasks, from routine observations of the effects of weightlessness to positioning

Below **The *Columbia* astronauts Jeffrey Hoffman, John Lounge, and Samuel Durrance demonstrate the behavior of a water bubble in the weightlessness of space. The astronauts' sleeping quarters can be seen in the background.**

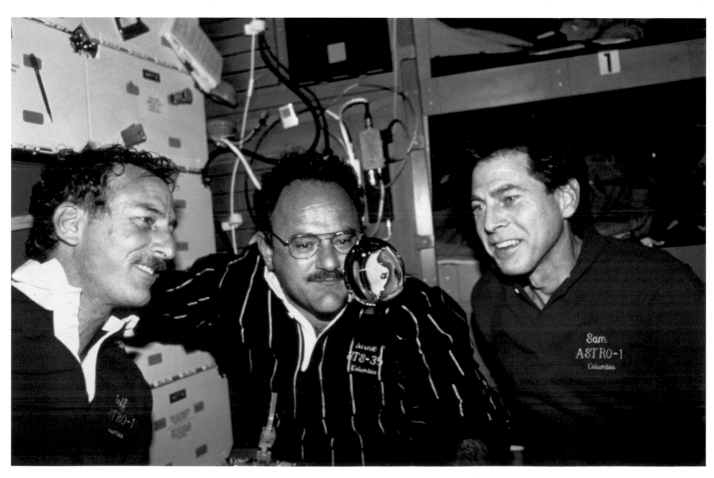

new satellites in orbit around the earth. The space shuttle carries pieces of equipment in its payload bay, which acts like the trunk of a car. Before takeoff, the payload bay is filled, and when the spacecraft leaves the earth's atmosphere, the astronauts open it and unload the cargo. In April 1990 the crew of the *Discovery* space shuttle launched the Hubble Space Telescope (HST) into orbit. In December 1993 the crew of *Endeavour,* another shuttle, performed an even more celebrated task when they completed a series of repairs to the HST.

While in space, astronauts conduct a number of scientific experiments designed for the benefit of people on earth. In preparation for longer space flights in the future—and perhaps for permanent extraterrestrial human habitats—astronauts also monitor the effects of zero gravity on their own body. Many suffer from a condition known as space sickness. It has also been noticed that, after spending long periods of time in space, astronauts grow slightly taller, the reason being that in space gravity does not compress the spine, as it does on earth.

Above **Taken in 1998 from the space shuttle** *Discovery,* **this photograph shows the** *Mir* **space station in orbit. Heavy thunderclouds can be seen above the earth's surface.**

Right **Sally Ride, seen here walking to the launch pad with the rest of the space shuttle crew in 1983, was the first American woman to travel in space.**

Becoming an Astronaut

NASA's first seven astronauts were pilots with engineering training and experience of flying aircraft. The selection process has since become much tougher. Pilot astronauts (those who operate spacecraft) must have a degree in engineering, biological science, physical science, or mathematics; they must have spent at least a thousand hours commanding a jet aircraft; they must be in good health; and their height must be between five feet, four inches and six feet, four inches (162.5–193 cm). Mission specialists (those who are responsible for shuttle operations) must be at least four feet, ten and a half inches (148.5 cm) tall. Each payload specialist must be qualified to carry out a particular highly specialized job or experiment.

After selection, it takes many months of training and study to become an astronaut. Simulators allow trainee astronauts to experience all aspects of spacecraft operations without leaving earth. Water tanks are used to mimic weightless conditions in space.

In 1983 Sally Ride became the first American woman in space. In an interview broadcast on the World Wide Web on March 23, 1999, she described what it was like to sleep in the orbiting space shuttle:

It's easy to go to sleep in space. It's easy to get very comfortable because you're just floating, but when you sleep all your muscles are relaxed, so in weightlessness your arms and legs automatically go into positions where the muscles are relaxed. That means that your arms float up in front of your face, so sleeping astronauts look like they're in a science-fiction movie.

Sally Ride

SEE ALSO

- Armstrong, Neil • Astronomical Instruments
- Astronomy • Clothing
- Communication Devices • Gagarin, Yury
- Glenn, John • NASA • Satellites
- Shepard, Alan B., Jr. • Solar System
- Spacecraft • Space Exploration

ASTRONOMICAL INSTRUMENTS

PROXIMA CENTAURI, the second closest star to Earth (after the Sun), lies at a distance of 4.22 light years, or around 25 trillion miles (40 trillion km) away. With the technology available at the beginning of the twenty-first century, it would take an astronaut many lifetimes to reach even this relatively close-by neighbor of earth. Unless the technology of space travel advances dramatically, exploration of outer space will continue to be conducted, as it always has been, by means of astronomical instruments.

Below **This engraving of Johannes Hevelius (1611–1687) depicts the astronomer using a quadrant to observe the stars; three clocks ensure accurate timekeeping.**

EARLY ASTRONOMICAL TOOLS

Viewed from the earth, the configuration of the stars in the sky changes according to the position of the observer. Thus, an accurate observation of celestial bodies is of enormous benefit to navigators seeking to establish their exact position in the absence of recognizable landmarks. Among the first celestial observation instruments was the astrolabe, invented in the sixth century BCE by Greek astronomers, developed by Arab astronomers during the Middle Ages, and used by European seafarers until the seventeenth century.

Marine astrolabes were used to calculate latitude (position north or south of the equator). The problem of calculating longitude (east-west position) at sea was solved between 1735 and 1761, when the English clock maker John Harrison developed the chronometer. Together, measurements of latitude and longitude give the exact position of an object or person on earth.

The quadrant and later the sextant were used to measure the angle of a given star above the horizon. More accurate than the astrolabe, the sextant in particular played a vital role in the charting of unexplored areas until it was finally superseded by radar technology in the 1940s and GPS (Global Positioning System) technology in the 1990s.

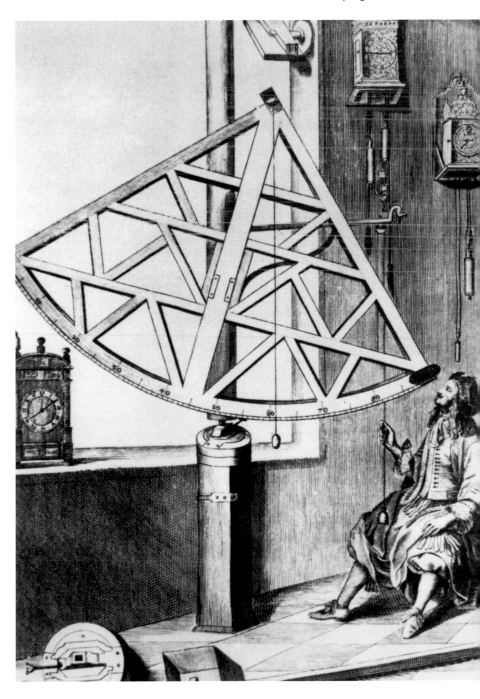

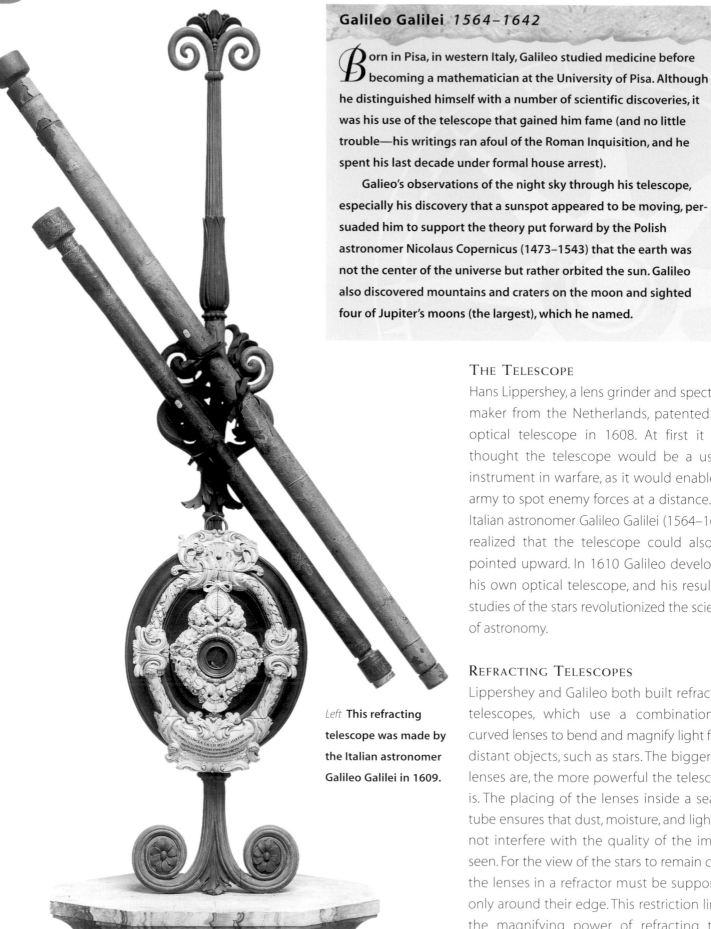

Galileo Galilei *1564–1642*

*B*orn in Pisa, in western Italy, Galileo studied medicine before becoming a mathematician at the University of Pisa. Although he distinguished himself with a number of scientific discoveries, it was his use of the telescope that gained him fame (and no little trouble—his writings ran afoul of the Roman Inquisition, and he spent his last decade under formal house arrest).

Galieo's observations of the night sky through his telescope, especially his discovery that a sunspot appeared to be moving, persuaded him to support the theory put forward by the Polish astronomer Nicolaus Copernicus (1473–1543) that the earth was not the center of the universe but rather orbited the sun. Galileo also discovered mountains and craters on the moon and sighted four of Jupiter's moons (the largest), which he named.

THE TELESCOPE

Hans Lippershey, a lens grinder and spectacle maker from the Netherlands, patented the optical telescope in 1608. At first it was thought the telescope would be a useful instrument in warfare, as it would enable an army to spot enemy forces at a distance. The Italian astronomer Galileo Galilei (1564–1642) realized that the telescope could also be pointed upward. In 1610 Galileo developed his own optical telescope, and his resulting studies of the stars revolutionized the science of astronomy.

REFRACTING TELESCOPES

Lippershey and Galileo both built refracting telescopes, which use a combination of curved lenses to bend and magnify light from distant objects, such as stars. The bigger the lenses are, the more powerful the telescope is. The placing of the lenses inside a sealed tube ensures that dust, moisture, and light do not interfere with the quality of the image seen. For the view of the stars to remain clear, the lenses in a refractor must be supported only around their edge. This restriction limits the magnifying power of refracting tele-

Left **This refracting telescope was made by the Italian astronomer Galileo Galilei in 1609.**

scopes, as very large lenses can warp under their own weight and thus distort the image. For this reason, refractors are not suitable for observing the far reaches of outer space (though they remain popular for observing celestial objects closer to earth).

REFLECTING TELESCOPES

In 1668, after noticing that images seen through refractors were often obscured by a surrounding halo of light, the English physicist Isaac Newton invented the reflecting telescope. Reflectors use mirrors to reflect light to a given point. Since light is bounced back and forth inside the tube, the tube itself can be shorter than that of a refractor. Also, as the mirrors may be supported across their entire width without distortion of the image, reflectors can be much larger—and therefore, more powerful.

SEEING FARTHER INTO SPACE

Images seen through earth-based optical telescopes are generally distorted by the earth's atmosphere. Air currents bend the light emitted from stars, and the artificial light produced by cities makes it difficult to see the dimmer objects in space. Astronomers have sidestepped these problems in a number of ways. Larger telescopes enable them to see farther. The positioning of telescopes in high places reduces the depth of the atmosphere the light has to pass through and the light pollution that is present at lower altitudes.

The largest single telescopes in the world, the identical Keck I and Keck II, are located on the summit of Mauna Kea, in Hawaii, at an altitude of 13,796 feet (4,145 m). Their reflective surface measures thirty-three feet (10 m) across and is made up of thirty-six hexagonal mirrors joined in a honeycomb pattern.

The Electromagnetic Spectrum

Through refractors, reflectors, and other optical telescopes, astronomers view the light wave energy that is visible. Objects also emit many forms of invisible wave energy, such as radio waves. The range of all wave energy is called the electromagnetic spectrum. By analyzing the electromagnetic energy emitted by extraterrestrial objects, astronomers can deduce the nature and position of those objects.

Radio Telescopes

In 1931 an American engineer named Karl Jansky discovered that interference in messages transmitted along telephone lines was caused by radio waves originating from outer space. In 1937 an amateur American astronomer by the name of Grote Reber built the first radio telescope and thereby inaugurated the science of radio astronomy, an entirely new way of studying the universe.

As radio waves have a much longer wavelength than visible light waves, a telescope with a much larger surface area is required to detect them. The world's largest radio telescope has a dish that measures one thousand feet (305 m) across and nestles in the hills of Arecibo, Puerto Rico. As radio telescopes are generally built outside, they can be adversely affected by the weather.

Among the phenomena revealed by radio telescopes is the dramatic landscape of the surface of Venus, concealed beneath dense cloud. Radio astronomy has greatly increased knowledge of the sun and the moon.

Below **The Very Large Array (VLA) radio telescope in New Mexico is the world's largest radio telescope array. Computers combine the data received by twenty-seven dish antennas, each eighty-two feet (25 m) in diameter.**

1608
Hans Lippershey patents the refracting telescope.

1609
Galileo first uses a telescope to observe the night sky.

1668
Isaac Newton invents the reflecting telescope.

1731
John Hadley designs a navigator's sextant.

1937
Grote Reber builds the first radio telescope.

1980
The Very Large Array observatory is constructed in New Mexico.

1990
The Hubble Space Telescope (HST) is put into orbit.

1993
Work begins on the Keck 1 telescope.

1993
Astronauts repair the Hubble Space Telescope.

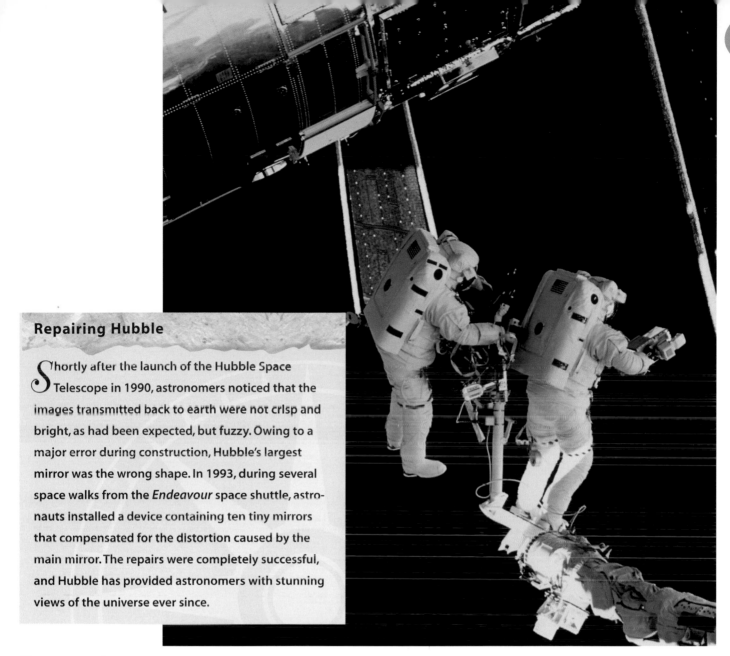

Repairing Hubble

Shortly after the launch of the Hubble Space Telescope in 1990, astronomers noticed that the images transmitted back to earth were not crisp and bright, as had been expected, but fuzzy. Owing to a major error during construction, Hubble's largest mirror was the wrong shape. In 1993, during several space walks from the *Endeavour* space shuttle, astronauts installed a device containing ten tiny mirrors that compensated for the distortion caused by the main mirror. The repairs were completely successful, and Hubble has provided astronomers with stunning views of the universe ever since.

TELESCOPE ARRAYS

As with optical telescopes, the larger the radio telescope is, the farther its reach. In 1980 the largest earth-based radio telescope, named the Very Large Array (VLA), was completed in Sorocco, New Mexico. Radio waves are received by a system of twenty-seven separate antennas, which can be moved along rails laid out in a Y shape. Two arms of the Y are 13 miles (21 km) long; the third measures 11.8 miles (19 km). Computers combine the data to form a single radio image.

SPACE TELESCOPES

Seen from space (without the interference of the earth's atmosphere), the view of the universe is much clearer. The apparent twinkling of the stars, for example, is caused by the light they emit being bent to and fro by the atmosphere. Viewed from space, starlight is bright and steady.

Launched in 1990, the Hubble Space Telescope (HST) captures images of space from its perpetual orbit, 372 miles (600 km) above the surface of the earth. Named after Edwin Hubble (1889–1953), the American astronomer who first provided evidence that the universe is expanding, HST picks up rays in the range between ultraviolet and infrared and provides images of exceptional clarity and detail.

Above **During a 1997 space walk to service HST, the astronaut Joseph Tanner, perched on the robot arm of the Remote Manipulator System, aims a camera at Hubble's solar panels while Gregory Harbaugh (left) assists.**

Right **An artist's impression of the James Webb Space Telescope, an instrument that will help astronomers study star, galaxy, and planet formation. The telescope's twenty-one-foot (6.5 m) mirror will be optimized to collect near- and mid-infrared radiation emitted billion of years ago, at a time when stars and planetary systems were being formed.**

JAMES WEBB SPACE TELESCOPE

Scheduled for launch around 2010, the James Webb Space Telescope (JWST) is named after NASA's second administrator. James Webb ran the organization from 1961 to 1968 and led the Apollo exploration program, which culminated in the first manned mission to the moon. JWST will spend three months traveling to its high orbit, around 930,000 miles (1.5 million km) from earth. At such a distance, it will not be possibe for JWST to be serviced by astronauts. Instead the petals of the telescope's mirror will be operated by remote control from earth.

JWST will be ten times as powerful as Hubble. A sun shield will keep the telescope cool as it collects data in the far-visible to mid-infrared part of the electromagnetic spectrum. Light from stars and galaxies in the depths of space have stretched into longer, redder wavelength bands by the time their light reaches the solar system. It is hoped that the new telescope's improved infrared vision will allow astronomers to study the origins of galaxies, stars, and planets.

On September 10, 2002, Sean O'Keefe, the NASA administrator, announced the newly chosen name for the successor to the Hubble Space Telescope:

It is fitting that Hubble's successor be named in honor of James Webb. Thanks to his efforts, we got our first glimpses at the dramatic landscape of outer space. He took our nation on its first voyages of exploration, turning our imagination into reality. Indeed, he laid the foundations at NASA for one of the most successful periods of astronomical discovery. As a result, we're rewriting the textbooks today with the help of the Hubble Space Telescope, the Chandra X-ray Observatory, and, in 2010, the James Webb Telescope.

SEE ALSO

- Astronauts • Astronomy • Chronometer
- NASA • Navigational Instruments • Satellites
- Solar System • Spacecraft • Space Exploration

ASTRONOMY

ASTRONOMY IS THE STUDY OF OBJECTS AND MATTER that lie outside the earth's atmosphere. Without leaving the earth, astronomers explore the universe and observe how planets, stars, and other extraterrestrial phenomena are formed, how they evolve, what they are made of, how they move, and the distance between them. From the early days of exploration until the twentieth century, navigators, especially those traveling by sea, were also required to be amateur astronomers: in the absence of recognizable landmarks, the only sure way to determine one's position was by analyzing the stars.

PICTURING THE UNIVERSE

In the second century CE the Greek astronomer Ptolemy formulated a geocentric (earth-centered) view of the universe. According to Ptolemy, all celestial bodies (the sun, moon, planets, and stars) travel in circles around a stationary earth. The Ptolemaic picture of the universe remained largely unchallenged until the sixteenth century, when Nicolaus Copernicus (1473–1543), a Polish priest and astronomer, put forward an alternative theory, that the earth and planets revolve around the sun and, moreover, that the earth rotates on its own axis every day. Copernicus was not correct in every respect. According to his heliocentric (sun-centered) system, the sun is the center of the whole universe, and the planets (which Copernicus thought equal in size) orbit in perfect circles.

Later in the century, a Danish astronomer, Tycho Brahe (1546–1601), made the most accurate astronomical observations to that date. Using Brahe's research, his student Johannes Kepler (1571–1630), a German, advanced astronomy in a number of ways, especially with his discovery that planetary orbits are not circular but elliptical (oval).

Early in the seventeenth century the Italian astronomer Galileo Galilei (1564–1642) pioneered the use of telescopes to study the night sky. Though Galileo's observations revealed the existence of sunspots and much else formerly unknown, he scoffed at Kepler's theory of elliptical orbits and tried to explain planetary motion in terms of multiple patterns of circular movement. Isaac Newton's laws of motion, published in 1687, finally provided a unifying theory to describe the movement of all objects in the universe.

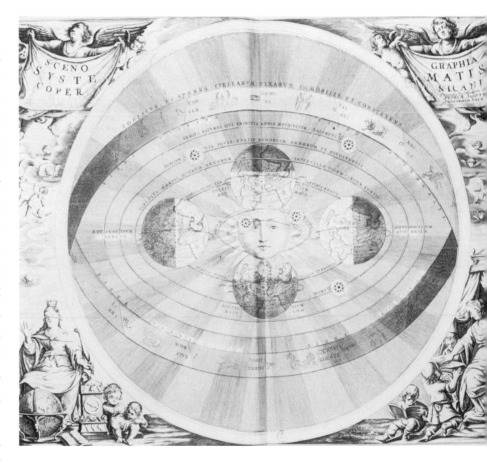

bove **This engraving of the Copernican system, part of a 1660 work titled** *Harmonia Macrocosmica,* **places the sun at the center of the universe.**

NEWTON AND GRAVITY

The English physicist and mathematician Isaac Newton (1642–1727) revolutionized the study of astronomy. While still a student he directed a beam of white light through a glass prism. The light was separated into a rainbow (or spectrum) of visible colors, each refracted (bent) to a different degree according to its wavelength. This discovery laid the groundwork for later studies of the electromagnetic spectrum, the range of all energy waves emitted by objects. Newton also invented the reflecting telescope. Built using mirrors rather than lenses, this instrument eliminated the fuzzy halo that surrounded images when viewed through a refracting telescope (the kind used by Galileo).

Newton's most significant contribution to astronomy lay in his studies of planetary motion. According to legend, after watching an apple fall from a tree, he was struck by the concept of gravity. Deducing that a force had pulled the apple toward the earth, he went on to conclude that all objects, from apples to planets, are subject to gravity. From this starting point Newton elaborated on his laws of motion to explain why planets maintain their orbit around the sun instead of spinning off into space.

EINSTEIN AND RELATIVITY

At the beginning of the twentieth century, many of the celestial phenomena observed by astronomers over the course of several centuries still remained unexplained. The

Above **The discovery that objects emit a range of energy of different wavelengths began with Newton's separation of white light.**

c. 300 BCE
The Greek astronomer Aristarchus of Samos suggests that the earth spins on its own axis and revolves around the sun.

c. 245 BCE
The Greek mathematician Eratosthenes calculates the polar circumference of the earth.

c. 129 BCE
The Greek astronomer Hipparchus compiles the first catalog of stars.

1543 CE
Nicolaus Copernicus argues that the earth revolves around the sun.

1609
Johannes Kepler argues that planetary orbits are elliptical (oval); Galileo first studies the stars through a telescope.

1687
Newton describes the force of gravity in *Principia Mathematica*.

1781
William Herschel discovers the planet Uranus.

Newton's Laws of Motion

*F*irst published in 1687, Newton's three laws of motion state the principles behind the movement of all objects in the universe. They may be summarized as follows:

1. Every object remains in a state of rest or in a state of motion at constant speed in a straight line unless an external force is applied to it.
2. The acceleration of an object is proportional to the force applied to it and takes place in the direction in which the force is exerted.
3. For every action, there is an equal and opposite reaction.

Right **Isaac Newton was knighted by Queen Anne in 1705, the first occasion on which a scientist had been so honored.**

German physicist Albert Einstein (1879–1955), with his special theory of relativity (1905) and general theory of relativity (1916), gave scientists an all-inclusive way of thinking about space, time, and gravitation. Several expeditions were sent out to observe the 1919 solar eclipse, and the resulting photographs of stars near the sun bore out Einstein's theories. Einstein transformed the Newtonian picture of the universe, and for his invaluable contribution to science, he was awarded the Nobel Prize for physics in 1921.

1820
The Royal Astronomical Society is founded in London.

1846
The planet Neptune is seen for the first time.

1916
Albert Einstein publishes his general theory of relativity.

1929
Edwin Hubble suggests that the universe is expanding.

1930
The planet Pluto is discovered.

1931
Karl Jansky intercepts radio waves from the Milky Way.

APRIL 1990
The Hubble Space Telescope is launched.

Above **This photograph of the Milky Way shows the bright star clusters at the center of the galaxy, 30,000 light years away.**

STARS

Stars are bodies of gas, mostly hydrogen and helium, that radiate immense amounts of energy in the form of visible light, infrared light, heat, and radio waves. Galaxies, spinning groups of millions of stars, are in turn grouped together in clusters. The earth's solar system is part of the Milky Way, a spiral galaxy that contains 100 billion stars.

One of the most significant contributors to the study of the stars was the British astronomer William Herschel (1738–1822), court astronomer to King George III. Using telescopes he made himself and aided in his observations by his sister Caroline Lucretia (1750–1848), Herschel cataloged a number of new stars and gained celebrity status when he discovered Uranus, a previously unknown planet. Herschel was among the first astronomers to suggest that the cosmos was dynamic rather than unchanging.

Observed from the earth with the naked eye, stars appear to be uniformly white, whereas they are in fact different colors, according to their temperature. Stars have a lifetime, during which they evolve through many different stages of mass, heat, color, and luminosity (brightness), each lasting perhaps trillions of years.

The end state of a star's life may be dramatic. Some shrink into dwarf stars and burn themselves out. Others shrink into neutron stars, with a mass around one million times greater than that of dwarf stars packed into an area perhaps twelve miles (20 km) across. Spinning neutron stars are known as pulsars; they emit radio waves that can be detected on earth. Some stars explode violently into supernovas, with a luminosity millions or billions of times the star's original luminosity. Some stars implode (collapse inward) and form a point of zero volume and infinite mass: a black hole. The gravitational pull of a black hole would be so strong that any body approaching one or a ray of light directed at one would be sucked in and unable to escape.

In fact, neutron stars, pulsars, black holes, and a host of other astronomical phenomena are hypothetical: that is to say, they have never been directly detected; their presence is merely inferred from their effect on neighboring objects. One of the more mysterious constituents of the universe is so-called dark matter, which has never been detected but is believed by many astrophysicists to make up as much as 90 percent of the mass of the universe.

OTHER ASTRONOMICAL PHENOMENA

Quasars, first discovered by astronomers in 1963, are tiny starlike objects in the farthest reaches of space. Modern astronomers believe quasars are the bright cores of distant galaxies. Comets are balls of frozen rock that orbit the sun along sweeping elliptical paths. When a comet passes closer to the sun, solar radiation causes it to trail a long tail of dust behind it. The name *comet* comes from the Greek *kometes* ("hairy one"). Asteroids are pieces of rock that orbit the sun. Meteoroids are smaller rocks that often burn up when they enter the earth's atmosphere. A meteoroid that falls to earth is called a meteorite.

Below The appearance of Halley's comet at the Battle of Hastings (1066) was thought of as an ill omen. King Harold of England was later killed in battle.

Right **The one-thousand-foot (305 m) Arecibo radio telescope in Puerto Rico is used by SETI (Search for Extraterrestrial Intelligence), an organization that searches for evidence of life elsewhere in the universe.**

THE FUTURE OF ASTRONOMY

In 2002 astronomers predicted that an asteroid could be on course to hit the earth in the year 2880. While the earth has survived the impact of small meteorites, a large asteroid impact would be catastrophic. It is possible that around sixty-five million years ago an asteroid measuring some 6.2 miles (10 km) across and traveling at hundreds of thousands of miles per hour smashed into eastern Mexico. Some experts argue that the global environmental disaster that followed caused the extinction of the dinosaurs.

The possibility that life may exist elsewhere in the universe has long been a source of intrigue. Since 1960 astronomers have been monitoring radio waves from space in the hope of detecting extraterrestrial intelligence. In the future astronomers may help determine whether humans will be able to survive permanently on other planets.

Most astronomers subscribe to the big bang theory, according to which the universe was created in an enormous explosion. However, what existed before the big bang remains a mystery. As for the long-term future, beyond a general process of expansion, it remains unclear what lies ahead for the universe. Astronomers continue to search for the answers.

The American astronomer and Pulitzer Prize–winning writer Carl Sagan (1934–1996) believed in a strong connection between humans and the universe.

The universe forces those who live in it to understand it. Those creatures who find everyday experience a muddled jumble of events with no predictability, no regularity, are in grave peril. The universe belongs to those who, at least to some degree, have figured it out.

Carl Sagan, *Broca's Brain: Reflections on the Romance of Science*

SEE ALSO

- Astronauts • Astronomical Instruments
- Eratosthenes of Cyrene • Hipparchus
- NASA • Ptolemy • Satellites
- SETI (Search for Extraterrestrial Intelligence)
- Solar System • Space Exploration

AUDUBON, JOHN JAMES

KNOWN AS THE AMERICAN WOODSMAN, JOHN JAMES AUDUBON (born Jean Fougère Rabin in 1785) was the best-known painter of American birds and animals in the nineteenth century. Audubon, who journeyed deep into the wilderness to record his subjects, is famous for his impressive collection of color illustrations, entitled *Birds of America* and published between 1827 and 1838. He died in 1851, and in 1886 his work was honored with the formation of the U.S National Audubon Society, which continues to protect American bird life and its habitats.

EARLY LIFE AND MARRIAGE

John James Audubon was born in Santo Domingo, Haiti, the son of a French plantation owner and his mistress. Audubon spent his childhood in Nantes in France and at fourteen was sent to the military academy at Rochefort. He may also have spent some time in Paris in 1802 as a student under Jacques-Louis David, the great French Revolutionary artist. Audubon's family's fortune was lost following slave revolts in Santo Domingo. In 1803 Audubon sailed to America, where his father owned a farm at Mill Grove, near Philadelphia. There the younger Audubon met an English girl, named Lucy Bakewell, who married him in 1808 and supported him through all his later financial difficulties.

After a few months of happiness at Mill Grove, Audubon's fortunes began to flounder. In 1805 he was swindled out of the profits from the lead mines on his estate. A dangerous voyage to warring France nearly cost him his life when the crew of a British privateer (a government-licensed pirate ship) took him captive at sea in April 1806. After the failure of several other business ventures, the Mill Grove estate had to be sold.

Right **Though portrayed as a hunter in this portrait by his son, Audubon fought to protect wildlife.**

RELUCTANT SHOPKEEPER

In the summer of 1807, Audubon set off with a friend by the name of Ferdinand Rozier, intending to make his fortune in the West. After a thousand-mile (1,600 km) journey by stagecoach and flatboat, Audubon settled in Louisville, Kentucky, and set up a store with Rozier.

Audubon, however, was a reluctant shopkeeper and spent all of his spare time hunting and drawing the birds that lived along the banks of the Ohio, Mississippi, and lower Missouri Rivers. Rozier eventually grew tired of his business partner, and in 1809, after several failed attempts at setting up his own business, Rozier left Audubon.

For the next eleven years, Audubon was involved in a number of businesses, first independently and later with his brother-in-law. Despite the failure of these business pursuits, Lucy Audubon stood by her husband. Though practically penniless, Audubon never gave up drawing, even after a family of rats ruined many of his pictures. From 1820 to 1825, Audubon funded his painting by teaching in Kentucky and Tennessee while Lucy raised the family and taught part time. In 1827 Lucy's patience finally paid off when, during a trip to London, Audubon secured a contract for the publication of his remarkable drawings of American birds.

Right **Audubon's extremely popular works were among the first to depict animals, such as this black-footed ferret, in natural contexts.**

1785
John James Audubon is born in Haiti.

1803
Sails to America to manage his father's estate.

1804
Conducts his first bird-banding experiments.

1807
Makes first voyage to the American interior.

1820
Explores the Mississippi River and sketches birds indigenous to the area.

1826
Sails to Britain in search of a publisher.

1827
Publishes first plates of *Birds of America*.

1832
Explores the palmetto groves of Florida.

1833
Visits the coast of Labrador, in eastern Canada.

1843
Travels up the Missouri River from Saint Louis to Nebraska.

Bird Banding

Audubon spent much of his time at Mill Grove hunting and drawing birds. He also began to study their habits and, in the spring of 1804, carried out the first recorded bird-banding experiments in the Americas. His technique consisted of tying distinctive silver threads to the legs of nestling Eastern Phoebes (or peewees) that were living in a cave on the bank of the Perkiomen River, in eastern Pennsylvania. With the return of the banded birds the following year, Audubon's experiment established that this particular species returns to the same nesting site each year. Audubon conducted his banding experiments more than a hundred years before the U.S. Bird Banding Society was launched.

WILDIFE OF THE SOUTH AND WEST

Journeys to South Carolina, Florida, and Labrador in the early 1830s gave Audubon the chance to observe and depict even more species. Having by that time acquired a certain amount of wealth, Audubon could afford to plan an ambitious six-month expedition up the Missouri River. His intention was to record and draw the animal species of the American West.

In April 1843 Audubon set out from Saint Louis by steamship with the naturalist John Bachman. Audubon captured many specimens and preserved them in barrels of rum in order to draw them later. While out west, however, he was horrified by the killing of vast numbers of buffalo on the prairies and was worried that overhunting might be driving many species of American mammals to extinction. Though Audubon had hoped to reach and cross the Rocky Mountains, he only managed to explore the upper Missouri and Yellowstone Rivers before it became necessary for him to return east. Three volumes of his book *Quadrupeds of North America* were published before he fell ill in the late 1840s. Years of overwork, much of it outdoors, had taken their toll. Audubon began to go blind and suffered a stroke in 1847. He died at his home in New York in 1851.

Birds of America

First published between 1827 and 1838, Audubon's most famous and successful work contained life-size drawings of wild birds, depicted vividly and dramatically. In 1807 Audubon had learned how to preserve and display dead birds at the museum of Dr. Samuel Mitchell in New York. The skills he picked up helped him to pose his models in lifelike and dramatic poses.

Audubon's first prints were published in Edinburgh in 1827. By the time the last was produced, eleven years later, Audubon had illustrated 1,065 species in 435 hand-colored plates. At almost the same time, from 1831 to 1839, Audubon worked with the Scottish naturalist William MacGillivray on the accompanying text, the five-volume *Ornithological Biographies*, which described the habits of the birds drawn by Audubon. The success of these two publications brought Audubon fame and riches. The original hand-colored plates are still prized by collectors. In 2000 a complete set was sold at auction in New York for the very large sum of almost nine million dollars.

ENDANGERED BIRDS

In the second half of the nineteenth century, after Audubon's death, feathers became a fashionable and popular adornment for ladies' accessories, especially hats. In order to meet the demand created by this fashion trend, hunters captured and killed millions of North American birds each year and sold their feathers to milliners (hat makers). Realizing that many species were in danger of extinction, in 1886 George Bird Grinnell set up an organization whose purpose was to

Above **Audubon's vivid drawing of the Carolina parakeet, from *Birds of America*.**

protect endangered birds. This organization eventually became the U.S. National Audubon Society, appropriately named after the man who revealed the variety and splendor of America's wildlife.

SEE ALSO

• Museums • Record Keeping

AVIATION

ONCE POWERED FLIGHT HAD BEEN DEVELOPED at the dawn of the twentieth century, progress in aviation technology was breathtakingly rapid. Within ten years, a plane had flown across the Atlantic Ocean. Within fifty years, jet aircraft were flying faster than the speed of sound. Though invented too late to be of major significance in the exploration of the earth, airplanes have nevertheless made an important contribution to humans' understanding of the planet.

4   L'Aéroplane "Blériot" en plein vol. — LL.

Left **Earthbound farmhands watch in amazement as the French aviation pioneer Louis Blériot flies by. In 1909, one year after this photograph was taken, Blériot became the first man to fly across the English Channel in an airplane.**

FIRST STEPS

The first flight in a motor-powered airplane was made by the American brothers Orville and Wilbur Wright in 1903. Yet humans had attained the goal of viewing the earth from the air much earlier. In China men were carried into the air strapped to kites as early as the sixth century CE. Balloon flight, pioneered in 1783 by the French brothers Joseph-Michel and Jacques Étienne Montgolfier, and glider flight, pioneered in 1853, also allowed people to view the earth from a far greater height than any building could provide at the time. Balloons were soon being used to make long-distance flights, such as the crossing of the English Channel in 1785. Early balloons were used mainly for reconnaissance in warfare rather than as vehicles for exploration.

EXPLORATION BY AIR

Although early flying machines were fragile and unreliable, the opportunity they offered to explore the areas of the world map that remained blank at the start of the twentieth century was too great to ignore. In the early years of the twentieth century, the largest unexplored regions of the earth were the

Arctic and the Antarctic, as well as vast tracts of the South American interior, especially the Amazon rain forest, and high mountainous regions, such as the Himalayas.

EXPLORING THE ARCTIC

The first airplane flight in the Arctic was made in August 1914, when the Polish pilot Jan Nagursky flew over the Barents Sea and the islands of Novaya Zemlya in search of marooned explorers. Although further exploratory flights were interrupted by World War I (1914–1918), aircraft and airships were widely used in the war, and aviation technology advanced considerably. Many polar explorers of the 1920s preferred the airplane and airship to skis and boats, which made slow and painful progress through the ice and freezing water.

On May 10, 1926, the American pilots Richard E. Byrd and Floyd Bennet claimed to have flown a Fokker monoplane to the North Pole. Two days later an international team, led by the American explorer Lincoln Ellsworth and his Norwegian counterpart Roald Amundsen, took the airship *Norge* to the Pole. Most polar historians are doubtful that Byrd and Bennet reached the Pole, but the *Norge* certainly did. In fact, given the doubt that also surrounds the navigation records of Robert E. Peary, who claimed in 1909 to have been the first man to reach the Pole on foot, it is possible that those aboard the *Norge* were the first humans to reach the North Pole by any means.

In any case, exploration by aircraft confirmed once and for all that there was no undiscovered continent within the Arctic Ocean and that, aside from a myriad desolate islands around its periphery, the top of the world was nothing more or less than a sea of frozen ice.

Below **In 1925 Roald Amundsen and Lincoln Ellsworth used this twin-engine seaplane to explore the Arctic.**

THE SECRETS OF ANTARCTICA

Antartica, the highest, coldest, and windiest continent on earth, is even more inaccessible than the Arctic; the first flight over Antarctica was not made until 1928. In December of that year, the Australian-born British pilot George Hubert Wilkins, together with the American Carl Ben Eielson, took off from Deception Island, in the South Shetlands, in a Lockheed Vega seaplane. They flew six hundred miles (970 km) south across Graham Land and discovered several new islands. Over the next two years the men mapped large portions of the southern polar region.

Balloons

*B*alloon travel is not for the fainthearted. The first balloons, made of stiffened paper, were lifted into the sky by hot air from a fire. The potentially lethal combination of paper and fire led to tragedy on several occasions. Another dangerous component of balloon (and airship) travel is hydrogen, a gas that is lighter than air and thus gives buoyancy to a canopy that is filled with it. Yet hydrogen is also a highly flammable gas. A single stray spark can all too easily cause a catastrophic inferno.

Balloons are difficult to steer. In 1897 a Swede named Salomon Andrée, together with two companions, attempted to take a balloon to the North Pole. Having set off from the island of Danskøya, part of the Spitsbergen archipelago (to the north of Norway), the men vanished into history. It was thirty years before their fate became known. In 1930 a seal-hunting ship found the men's bodies, together with their diaries and some photographs, on the island of Kritøya. A mere three days into their flight, 520 miles (830 km) from their starting point, Andrée and his companions had crashed onto the ice. After spending three harrowing months trying to get home, all three died of starvation and exposure.

Despite the invention of more reliable aircraft, balloons played a vital role in the exploration of the earth's atmosphere. In 1933 the Swiss-born Belgian Dr. Auguste Piccard set a world altitude record of 61,221 feet (18.7 km) in a hydrogen-filled balloon. Following this extraordinary flight high into the earth's stratosphere, Piccard's twin brother, Jean, predicted that steam-powered boats were a thing of the past. He declared, "the stratosphere is the superhighway of future intercontinental transport." His prediction proved accurate: the cruising altitude of modern passenger aircraft is in the calm air of the lower stratosphere.

Above **A huge crowd watches the Montgolfier brothers' first attempt at balloon flight. The brothers took off from the royal residence of Versailles in September 1783.**

Switching his attention from the North Pole to the South, Richard E. Byrd explored Antarctica from Little America, the base he set up on the ice shelf by the Bay of Whales. After making his first Antarctic flight on January 27, 1929, Byrd flew to the South Pole and back on November 29 of that year. Byrd made his journey in eighteen hours—a good deal less time than those who had preceded him on foot. Roald Amundsen had taken ninety-nine days. Robert Scott never returned.

Further exploratory flights were made by, among others, Lincoln Ellsworth and his Canadian copilot Herbert Hollick-Kenyon. The use of aircraft enabled the mapping of the interior of Antarctica to be completed within a remarkably short time period. Huge transport planes, such as the C-130, continue to make regular landings at the Scott-Amundsen Base at the South Pole, and journeys that once took months can be made in a matter of hours.

FILLING IN THE BLANKS

Away from the Poles, aircraft proved to be indispensable in the exploration and mapping of other parts of the world. An airplane flew over Mount Everest, the world's highest mountain, for the first time in 1933, when a tiny Westland biplane barely scraped over the summit. Advances in aviation technology were rapid, and it was not long before aerial photographs taken from above the Himalayas were being used to draw up detailed charts of the region.

1783
Balloon flight is pioneered by the Montgolfier brothers.

JANUARY 7, 1785
Jean-Pierre Blanchard and Dr. John Jeffries cross the English Channel in a balloon.

1897
Salomon Andrée sets off from Danskøya in an attempt to reach the North Pole by balloon.

1903
First powered flight is made by the Wright brothers.

1914
Jan Nagursky makes the first Arctic flight.

MAY 1926
Richard E. Byrd and Floyd Bennett reportedly fly to the North Pole; Lincoln Ellsworth and Roald Amundsen claim to have matched this achievement in the *Norge*.

1928–1930
Hubert Wilkins and Ben Eielson map Antarctica from the air.

1929
Richard E. Byrd flies to the South Pole and back.

Left **In 1933 this single-engine biplane became the first aircraft to fly over the summit of Mount Everest, the highest mountain in the world.**

Aerial Archaeology

*A*rchaeologists on the lookout for new sites to explore and excavate have pioneered a science known as aerial archaeology. Practitioners of this science are able to see from the air potential archaeological sites that are invisible from the ground. Stone Age villages, Roman villas, and ancient roads have all been discovered in this cost-effective way.

Structures buried underground, such as ditches, walls, building foundations, and burial sites, make their presence known by the subtlest of changes to the land above. There may be a slight rise in the ground that is only visible in shadow with low sunlight. When seen from above, this shadow might be laid out in a pattern that does not call attention to itself at the surface.

Certain crops, such as barley and wheat, grow differently if the soil in which they are planted is unlike the surrounding soil. A crop may grow taller or shorter or take on a different color. From the air an observer can detect shapes and patterns in crop growth that are invisible from the ground. Differences in the pattern and color of dead grass may also be related to the contents of the soil beneath. Aerial archaeologists also use satellite photographs and thermal and radar imaging techniques to unearth the secrets of the past.

1933
Airplanes fly over Mount Everest.

1971–1976
SLAR technology is used to map the Amazon basin.

2002
With a view to exploring Mars from the air, UAVs are tested on Devon Island.

EXPLORATION OF THE AMAZON BASIN

One of the last uncharted areas of the earth was the Amazon, an area of South American rain forest measuring some 900 million acres (3.64 million km²). Too vast and inaccessible to be mapped from the ground, the Amazon proved resistant even to standard aerial surveying, as cloud cover permanently obscures the land and makes photography redundant. A solution was found in the 1970s, with the development of SLAR (side-looking airborne radar) technology. A radar array mounted sideways on a plane sends out radio waves, analyzes the returning echoes, and builds a scan of the designated area. The shape of the land is revealed regardless of weather or light conditions.

The aerial exploration of the Amazon has, unfortunately, opened the door to those who wish to exploit the resources of the region. The size of the rain forest shrinks year by year as vast areas are deforested to make way for profitable cattle pasture. The loss to humanity—through the elimination of peoples for whom the rain forest is a livelihood, the extinction of never-discovered species, and

Right **Aircraft have made the exploration of the vast Amazon rain forest, which covers this stretch of impenetrable terrain in eastern Ecuador, far easier than it formerly was.**

Mars from the Air

One possible method of exploring Mars will be to use radio-controlled airplanes, known as UAVs (unmanned aerial vehicles). Such vehicles have been tested over Devon Island in the Arctic, whose rocky, icy, crevasse-marked terrain is similar to that of Mars. UAVs are small and lightweight but have a comparatively large wingspan of fifty-six feet (17 m), an essential component if they are to remain airborne in Mars's thin atmosphere. UAVs would be delivered to the surface of the planet aboard a landing craft and then assembled, possibly by astronauts.

At the beginning of the twenty-first century, knowledge of the surface of Mars was provided by photographs taken by orbiting satellite and remote-controlled land vehicles, which have surveyed a minute section of the surface. UAVs would be effective for speedy exploration, as they could fly several times over interesting regions and take photographs of the same area from different angles. On the other hand, satellites take shots only looking straight down from a great height.

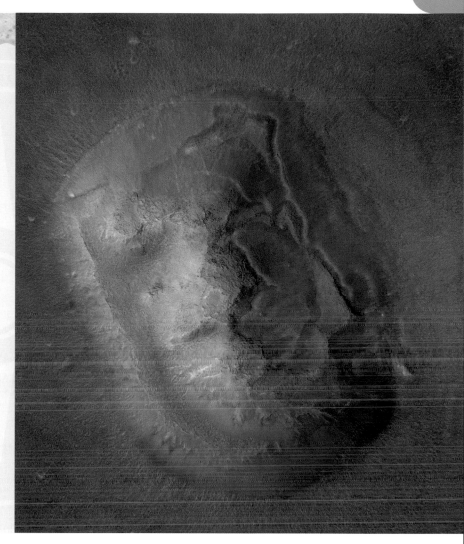

the dangerous disturbance of the ecological balance of the world—is incalculable.

MODERN USES OF AVIATION IN EXPLORATION

Aerial surveying is widely used to update maps that were originally drawn up using ground-surveying techniques. Most countries are routinely photographed at least once a decade. Aerial photographs can be used to check the accuracy of a map, and infrared or ultraviolet lenses can reveal details not recorded by natural-light photography.

The major drawback of aerial photography is that the lens of a camera tends to distort the image it conveys to the film. Ordinarily, this distortion presents no problem, especially in a standard shot of a group of people or a building. However, what would be an imperceptible distortion in an ordinary photograph becomes a noticeable error in an image taken from the sky of many square miles of land, especially around the edge of the shot. Other image-recording techniques used in aerial surveying, such as sonar, radar, and seismic measurement, are more accurate. Such non-photographic techniques can also reveal features invisible to the human eye and to the natural-light camera—for example, the floor of the ocean.

SEE ALSO
- Amundsen, Roald • Byrd, Richard E.
- Ellsworth, Lincoln • Land Transport
- Peary, Robert E. • Polar Exploration
- Remote Sensing

Above **This extraordinary shot, taken by the Mars Global Surveyor (MGS) in 2001, shows a mountainous area around a mile (1.6 km) across in the Cydonia region of Mars. The photo was taken from a height of 280 miles (450 km).**

Above **In 1616 Baffin sailed past Sanderson's Hope, a cliff on the eastern side of Baffin Bay. The cliff was named in 1587 by John Davis in honor of the chief backer of his expedition, William Sanderson, whose hope was to find the Northwest Passage.**

In 1616 Baffin reflected on his own wasted efforts in search of the passage:

How many of the best sort of men have set their endeavours to prove a passage that way! Yes. What great sums of money have been spent on it! . . . How vain the best and chiefest hopes of men are in things uncertain!

Quoted in George Malcolm Thomson, *The North-West Passage*

The following year, on a second voyage in search of the passage, Baffin and Bylot sailed up Davis Strait until they reached a bay, later named Baffin Bay. They discovered a small opening to the west, which they named Lancaster Sound; they were prevented from exploring the sound because it was late in the year and ice was beginning to block the entrance. Unaware that Lancaster Sound is the start of the true Northwest Passage, Baffin returned to London with the disappointing (but incorrect) news that there was "no passage nor hope of a passage in the north of Davis Straits."

FINAL YEARS

After giving up the search for the passage, Baffin served as a navigator in the Indian Ocean. In 1622 he was part of an English force supporting the shah of Persia (present-day Iran) in the shah's efforts to drive the Portuguese out of the Persian Gulf. On April 23, 1622, Baffin took part in an attack on a castle on the island of Qeshm. According to the scholar Samuel Purchas, Baffin "received a shot from the castle into his belly, wherewith he gave three leaps, and died immediately."

SEE ALSO
- Hudson, Henry • Latitude and Longitude
- Navigational Instruments
- Northwest Passage

BANKS, JOSEPH

THE INFLUENTIAL ENGLISH NATURALIST JOSEPH BANKS (1743–1820) sailed on James Cook's first voyage around the world (1768–1771). The animal and plant specimens he gathered would later form the basis of the collection of the Natural History Museum in London. In later life Banks organized expeditions to many of Britain's new colonies. He served as president of the Royal Society from 1778 until his death in 1820.

EARLY SUCCESS

Joseph Banks was born into a wealthy family that owned large estates in Lincolnshire, in eastern England. After he inherited his fortune in 1761, Banks was free to spend time and money on botany, a passion since his youth. In 1766 he became the youngest person to be elected a fellow of the Royal Society, Britain's most prestigious scientific organization. From 1766 to 1767 he traveled to Labrador and Newfoundland, in northeastern Canada, and collected animal, plant, and rock specimens. In 1768 Banks persuaded the Admiralty and the Royal Society to allow him to join James Cook's *Endeavour* voyage.

NEW DISCOVERIES IN THE PACIFIC

Although the chief scientific purpose of Cook's expedition was to witness the transit of Venus, the men's tasks also included recording the plants and animals of any lands the party encountered. At his own expense, Banks put together a team of eight assistants, including the illustrator Sydney Parkinson and the Swedish botanist Daniel Solander.

The expedition traveled to the Pacific via the Atlantic island of Madeira, Rio de Janeiro (Brazil), and Tierra del Fuego (Argentina), where Banks and Solander made significant plant collections. The party successfully observed the transit of Venus from Tahiti on June 3, 1769, and Banks made extensive notes

not only on the flora and fauna but also on the peoples he encountered. Banks was especially impressed by the intricate tattoo designs that were worn by many of the peoples of the Polynesian islands.

Above **For his contribution to science and exploration, Joseph Banks was knighted in 1781.**

On the east coast of Australia, Banks and his assistants spent eight days (at a place later named Botany Bay) amassing a huge collection. They returned home in 1771 with over 1,300 new species of plants, 500 new species of birds and fish, and too many insects to count. Banks's report on the voyage was a huge popular success, particularly for its descriptions of unfamiliar creatures, such as the kangaroo and the koala.

LANDMARKS IN BOTANY

After a 1772 expedition to the Hebrides Islands and Iceland, places that were not well known to the British scientific community, Banks made no further voyages himself. He nevertheless offered vital support to other expeditions—notably the voyage of the *Bounty* to the South Pacific in 1787, during which botanists attempted to transplant

Pacific breadfruit to plantations in the West Indies in order to provide food for slaves.

In 1773 Banks was appointed director of the Royal Botanic Gardens at Kew, west of London. His home became a meeting place for botanists from around the world. Banks gave generous support to botanical collectors planning to explore new lands. As a member of the African Association, he helped the Scottish explorer Mungo Park (1771–1806) to travel to West Africa and the English botanist Alan Cunningham (1791–1839) to visit South America and Australia. In all, Banks sponsored more than a dozen major expeditions and oversaw the arrival of hundreds of new specimens at Kew.

BANKS AND AUSTRALIA

During his voyage with Cook, Banks had been impressed by the lands around Botany Bay, in

Below **Under Banks's supervision, Kew Gardens became the world's most important center for the collection and study of botanical specimens.**

Benjamin Thompson *1753–1814*

The inventor Benjamin Thompson was born in Massachusetts and fled to Europe in 1776 after the start of the American Revolution. In 1784 he was knighted for his military services in America and for his experiments with gunpowder. Thompson spent the next fifteen years modernizing the German state of Bavaria. He reformed the Bavarian army, drained the marshes around the town of Mannheim, and improved farming methods. For these services he was ennobled as Count Rumford of the Holy Roman Empire. Thompson was a friend of Joseph Banks, and in 1799 the two men founded the Royal Institution of Great Britain to promote public interest in science. Thompson invented many practical devices, such as improved chimneys, a kitchen range for cooking, and a drip coffeepot.

Above **The American-born inventor Benjamin Thompson was honored by several countries.**

eastern Australia (a country then known as New Holland). In the belief that the new continent could be settled, he urged the British government to send convicts to establish a British colony in New Holland. In honor of this vision and in honor of Banks's efforts to encourage the exploration of Antarctica, the Swedish botanist Carolus Linnaeus suggested that New Holland be renamed Banksia. Although this suggestion was never adopted (the name Australia was chosen in 1830), in 1793 Banks's name was given to a group of volcanic islands in the South Pacific near the island of Vanuatu.

SEE ALSO
- Cook, James
- Exploration and Geographical Societies
- Flinders, Matthew • Natural Sciences
- Park, Mungo

FEBRUARY 13, 1743
Joseph Banks is born.

1766
Is elected a fellow of the Royal Society; travels to Newfoundland and Labrador.

1768–1771
Sails with James Cook to the South Pacific.

1772
Sails to the Hebrides and Iceland.

1773
Becomes director of Kew Botanical Gardens.

1778
Is made president of the Royal Society; helps found the African Association.

1781
Is knighted by King George III.

1787
Organizes the expedition of HMS *Bounty*.

1801
Sponsors Matthew Flinders's voyage around Australia.

1804
Founds the London Horticultural Society.

1820
Dies.

Belalcázar, Sebastián de

SEBASTIÁN DE BELALCAZÁR (c. 1495–1551) rose from humble beginnings to become a conquistador of great ambition and widespread fame. In the process of conquering considerable areas of present-day Ecuador and Colombia, he explored a large expanse of northwestern South America. Despite his success, Belalcázar's single-mindedness and ruthlessness made him unpopular, and his career ended in disgrace.

Below **An engraving of Sebastián de Belalcázar, one of many conquistadores who searched fruitlessly for El Dorado.**

Sebastián de Belalcázar (whose name may also be spelled Benalcázar) was born in the southern Spanish town of Belalcázar. Although he was baptized Sebastián Moyano, from the time he arrived in the New World, he ceased using his family name. He may have taken this action because his family, whose members were numbered among the lower Spanish nobility, had been involved in a feud with other noble families in Spain. Consequently, in the Spanish territories in Central and South America, he came to be known by the name of the town of his birth.

THE CONQUEST OF NICARAGUA

In 1519 Belalcázar decided to join the wave of Spanish settlers seeking their fortune in the New World. Having trained as a soldier, he joined the forces of the elderly nobleman Pedro Arias Dávila (c.1440–1531), the governor of the new Central American Spanish colony of Darién (in present-day Panama). When an expedition was commissioned to explore and conquer the nearby area of present-day Nicaragua in 1522, Belalcázar played a prominent role and earned a reputation as a gallant fighter in battles against the native peoples.

PERU AND ECUADOR

On two journeys along the Pacific coast of South America, in 1524 and 1526, the Spanish conquistador Francisco Pizarro had learned of a rich and powerful Incan empire, said to be centered on the town of Cuzco (in present-day southeastern Peru). Pedro Arias Dávila, Pizarro's superior, forbade any attempt to be made on the Incas because he was unwilling to bear the cost in men and materials. Undeterred, however, Pizarro went to Spain, where King Charles I himself sanctioned the

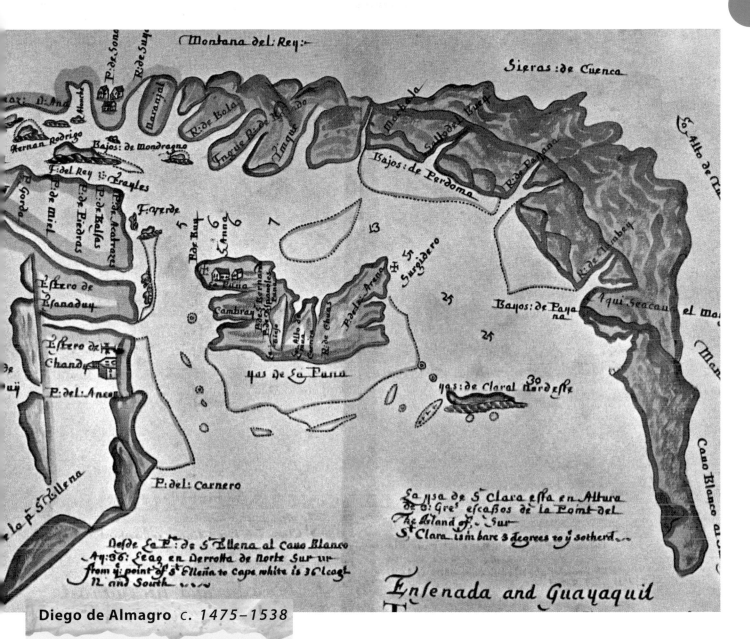

Within the map, the following labels appear:

Montana del: Rey:-

Sieras :de Cuenca

Bajos: de Mondragno

Bajos: de Perdoma

Bajos: de Pana na

yas de La Puna

yas: de Clara Nordesse

P: del: Carnero

La ysa de S. Clara essa en Altura de o: Gres escaßos de la Eomt del The Island of - Sur S. Clara ism bare 3 degrees to y sotherd.

Desde La P: de S. Ellena al Cauo Blanco Ay: 36: Leag en Derrotta de Norte Sur ur from y point of S. Ellena to Cape white is 36 leag. N. and South

Enfenada and Guayaquil

Diego de Almagro c. 1475–1538

Having run away to become a soldier at the age of fifteen, Diego de Almagro arrived in the New World in 1514. He played a key role in Francisco Pizarro's conquest of the Incan Empire and lost an eye and several fingers in combat with Indians. Having fallen out with Pizarro, in 1534 Almagro embarked on an expedition along the central Andes Mountains and into present-day Chile. On his return to Peru, he became engaged in civil wars among the rival Spanish settlers. Pizarro defeated Almagro in a battle at Salinas and executed him shortly afterward.

conquest of the Incas. Pizarro's ships left Panama in 1531, with Belalcázar among the company.

Belalcázar was given the task of maintaining the Spanish base on the coast at Piura, while Pizarro and Diego de Almagro marched inland toward the centers of Incan power. Belalcázar decided to mount a campaign of his own. With himself at the head of a small force, he followed the Inca road north to the city of Quito (the present-day capital of Ecuador), which he conquered and entered on December 6, 1534. Belalcázar then established a new city at Guayaquil and set up the port of Guayaquil on the Pacific coast.

Above **Depicted in the upper left hand corner of this seventeenth-century Spanish map of the Gulf of Guayaquil is the port of Guayaquil, established by Belalcázar in 1535 and now part of Ecuador.**

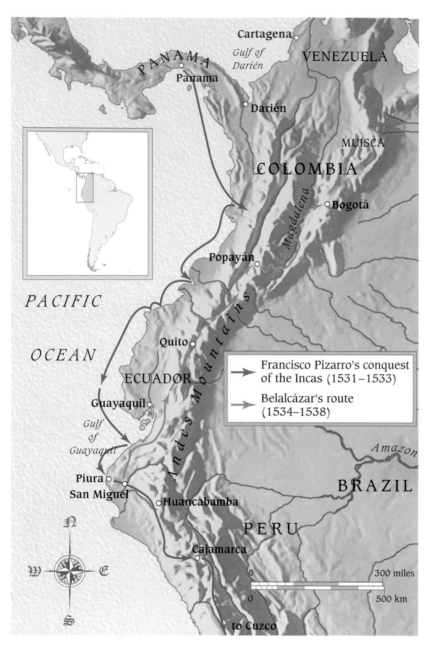

became known, was Louis de Daza, one of Belalcázar's officers. In 1535 Belalcázar gathered a small force and marched north into the Andes Mountains in search of El Dorado.

As the men made slow progress north into the Popayán district of present-day Colombia, they endured many hardships and encountered not a golden kingdom but other Spanish conquistadores. After the founding of the city of Popayán, relations between the rival adventurers became strained. In 1540 the party returned to Spain to request that the Council of the Indies decide who had the best claim to govern the new province. The council decided in favor of Belalcázar, who returned to the New World the following year as governor of Popayán.

DEATH AND ESTIMATION

Having left Spain an impoverished young man with no prospects of advancement, by 1541 Belalcázar was a celebrated conquistador and governor of a province that he himself had seized for the Spanish crown. From this high point in his career, however, his character and reputation began to decline. He ceased exploring and proved to be a poor administrator. His political skills were also found wanting when he became entangled in squabbles between various groups of Spanish administrators. Eventually, having ordered the execution of a neighboring governor, Jorge Robledo, Belalcázar himself was brought to trial and condemned to death. Back in Spain, the Council of the Indies agreed to hear Belalcázar's appeal, and he began the

Above **Having conquered Quito, Belalcázar pressed north but was frustrated in his desire to locate El Dorado.**

THE SEARCH FOR EL DORADO

Rumors soon reached Belalcázar of a kingdom, somewhere in the northern part of South America, fabulously rich in supplies of gold and silver. The first person to record the legend of El Dorado, as the mythical kingdom

---

c. 1495
Belalcázar is born Sebastián Moyano in southern Spain.

1519
Sails to the New World to seek his fortune.

1522–1531
Plays a prominent part in the conquest of Nicaragua.

1531
Begins conquest of Inca kingdom with Pizarro.

1534
Captures Quito.

1535
Founds city of Guayaquil; sets out to find El Dorado in region of modern Colombia.

1537
Founds city of Popayán.

1540
Returns to Spain and is recognized as governor of Popayán.

1551
Is sentenced to death; begins a journey back to Spain to appeal against the decision but dies at Cartagena, Colombia.

El Dorado

Legends of the golden kingdom of El Dorado may have their origin in an ancient custom of the Chibcha people, who ritually dusted their chief in gold powder and then washed him in a lake. (The name El Dorado, "the gilded man," referred originally to the king himself.) For a hundred years and more, European adventurers scoured northern South America for this promised land and, in doing so, explored and charted considerable areas of the Andes Mountains. Although wherever they went, explorers heard reports from local peoples that confirmed rumors of El Dorado, the farther they advanced, the farther El Dorado seemed to retreat. Fortune hunters continued to search for El Dorado into the seventeenth century, but no such place was ever found. The name (spelled Eldorado) survives only as the name of more than a dozen towns in the Americas—metaphorically it describes any alluring but unattainable goal.

long journey home. His case was never heard. Exhausted and dispirited, he died of fever at Cartagena, on the coast of Colombia.

SEE ALSO

• Núñez de Balboa, Vasco
• Spain

Left **The Incan god represented in this golden carving is adorned with a semicircular crown and holds a cup and corncob, symbols of food and drink.**

BELL, GERTRUDE

GERTRUDE BELL WAS BORN IN COUNTY DURHAM in northeastern England in 1868 and died in Baghdad, the Iraqi capital, in 1926. She was a prominent and highly respected figure in the British administration in Iraq after World War I. Known for her passion for Iraq, her archaeological journeys throughout the Middle East, and her lively letters and diaries, Bell was among the first European women to travel deep into the desert of Arabia.

Below **Gertrude Bell is pictured here next to Winston Churchill (left), then the British war minister, during the Cairo conference of 1921.**

BOLD TRAVELER

Gifted with an independent spirit and with enough money to pursue her desires, Bell chose a very different life from the path usually followed by young women in Victorian England. At age twenty-two she became the first woman to gain a first-class honors degree at the University of Oxford, where she studied modern history. After university, having discovered a passion for travel and adventure, she visited the Alps and proved to be an exceptional and fearless mountaineer. In 1897 and 1902 she made two trips around the world.

DAUGHTER OF THE DESERT

Bell's lifelong fascination with the Middle East dated from a visit to relatives in Persia (present-day Iran) in 1892. In the years that followed she learned Arabic and Persian and traveled extensively through Asia Minor (present-day Turkey), Syria, Arabia, and Mesopotamia (the ancient name for the area that became Iraq). Although the region was, at that time, relatively unexplored by Europeans, Bell, a tall, red-haired woman, chose to travel alone with only local guides (always men) to show her the region. In 1913 and 1914 she made a remarkable 1,500-mile (2,400 km) journey by camel across the Syrian Desert from Damascus (Syria) to Baghdad (Iraq) and back.

The following passage is excerpted from a letter Bell wrote to her parents during her travels in the Syrian desert:

We have come through all difficulties successfully; we have followed new roads the whole way and we have reaped a harvest that has surpassed the wildest flights of my imagination. I feel as if I had seen a whole new world and learnt several new chapters of history

From a letter written on April 5, 1909

Bell carried mapping equipment and a camera; her records enabled British surveyors to map the region more thoroughly, and her photographs of archaeological sites are a reminder of many places that have long since been destroyed by war or buried under sand.

Bell wrote lively letters home, translated Persian poetry, and kept journals. Her first book, *Persian Pictures*, was published in 1894, and in 1907 she wrote about Syria in *The Desert and the Sown*. *The Thousand and One Churches* (1909) presented her archaeological investigations in Asia Minor, while *Amurath to Amurath* (1911) described her groundbreaking journey in Mesopotamia.

Left **Bell poses on horseback in front of an Arabic funerary monument at Qubbet ed Duris, in Lebanon, in 1900.**

July 14, 1868
Gertrude Bell is born in County Durham, England.

1890
Graduates from Oxford University.

1892
Travels in Persia.

1897–1898
Makes first round-the-world trip.

1899–1902
Climbs in the Alps.

1905–1907
Takes part in archaeological excavations in Asia Minor.

1909
Follows the Euphrates River through Mesopotamia.

1913–1914
Travels from Damascus to Baghdad by camel.

1915
Joins the Arab Bureau in Cairo, Egypt.

1920
Becomes oriental secretary to the British High Commission in Iraq.

1921
Attends conference on the Middle East in Cairo; publishes *Review of the Civil Administration in Mesopotamia*.

1923
Founds archaeological museum in Baghdad.

July 12, 1926
Dies in Baghdad.

Bell's achievements earned respect for her, but being a woman did have social disadvantages:

Until quite recently I've been wholly cut off from [the Shias] because their tenets forbid them to look upon an unveiled woman and my tenets don't permit me to veil. . . . Nor is it any good trying to make friends through the women—if they were allowed to see me they would veil before me as if I were a man. So you see I appear to be too female for one sex and too male for the other.

From a letter written on March 14, 1920

KING MAKER

At the start of World War I (1914–1918), the British intelligence services valued Bell's knowledge of the Middle East very highly. In 1915 she was posted to Cairo, where, as an agent in the Arab Bureau, her task was to gather intelligence about the Ottoman Empire (an ally of Germany). After the war, the Allied powers divided Ottoman territories between them. Britain was given the mandate over Iraq, and Bell was made oriental secretary to the British High Commission there.

In 1921 Bell was consulted about the borders of the new nation of Iraq, as well as about the new ruler. She argued the case of Faisal I, who was crowned king later that year. She devoted the final years of her life to the creation of the National Museum of Iraq, which for the first time enabled artifacts excavated in Iraq to remain in Iraq. Bell died of a drug overdose in Baghdad in 1926. The National Museum remains a monument to her in the land she loved.

SEE ALSO

• Bishop, Isabella Lucy • Women and Exploration

Right **This plaque and bust are part of the collection of the National Museum of Iraq, Baghdad.**

GERTRUDE BELL
HER MEMORY
THE ARABS WILL ALWAYS HOLD
IN REVERENCE AND AFFECTION
SHE CREATED THIS MUSEUM IN 1923
BEING THEN
HONORARY DIRECTOR OF ANTIQUITIES
FOR THE IRAQ
WITH WONDERFULL KNOWLEDGE
AND DEVOTION SHE ASSEMBLED
THE MOST PRECIOUS OBJECTS IN IT
AND THROUGH THE HEAT
OF THE SUMMER WORKED ON THEM
UNTIL THE DAY OF HER DEATH
ON 12TH JULY 1926
KING FAISAL
AND THE GOVERNMENT OF IRAQ
IN GRATITUDE
FOR HER DEEDS IN THIS COUNTRY
HAVE ORDERED
THAT THE PRINCIPAL WING
SHALL BEAR HER NAME
AND WITH THEIR PERMISSION
HER FRIENDS
HAVE ERECTED THIS TABLET

GLOSSARY

aeronautics The study and practice of travel through the air.

Arikara Member of an American Indian people that lived by farming in circular dome-shaped earth lodges along the upper Missouri River.

black hole A hypothetical point in space of zero volume and infinite mass; the gravitational pull of a black hole is so strong that no object or light can escape from it.

colony A settlement or entire country governed by and owing allegiance to a mother country, which may be some distance away.

conquistador The Spanish word for "conqueror"; any of the soldiers, explorers, or settlers who, in the wake of Columbus's discovery of the Americas, helped to establish the Spanish presence in Central and South America during the sixteenth century.

electromagnetic spectrum The range of all known wave energy in the universe, including visible light, invisible light (such as infrared and ultraviolet), and radio waves.

extraterrestrial Referring to something whose origin is somewhere other than Earth.

gravity The fundamental physical force that one object exerts on another. The size of an object is the primary factor governing the gravitational force it exerts.

hemisphere Half of a sphere; specifically a half of the earth.

Inca Road The main north-south highway of the Incan Empire, which stretches some 4,350 miles (7,000 km) from Colombia to Chile and clings to the side of the Andes range at altitudes between 3,300 and 14,750 feet (1,000–4,500 m).

Inca A member of a people who ruled a large empire in northwestern South America from the thirteenth century until the sixteenth, when it fell to the Spanish conquistadores.

Louisiana Territory The land west of the Mississippi River, encompassing the drainage basins of the Missouri and Arkansas Rivers, purchased by President Thomas Jefferson from France in 1803.

militia An army unit formed of citizens, such as those used in early U.S. history by state governments.

Milky Way The galaxy of which Earth and its solar system are a part.

Oregon Trail A two-thousand-mile (3,220 km) path from Missouri to western Oregon, used from 1841 to the 1880s by thousands of settlers moving west.

Pacific Northwest The region of the present-day states of Washington and Oregon.

patent A government license giving an inventor the exclusive right to make or sell an invention for a certain number of years.

reconnaissance During armed conflict, the gathering of information on the movement and position of an enemy.

refractor A telescope that focuses light from distant objects through the use of glass lenses.

relativity The theory, first proposed by Einstein, that equated matter and energy by means of the speed of light, which Einstein believed was constant.

satellite An object, natural or artificial, that orbits a planet.

Sea of Tranquillity (in Latin, Mare Tranquilitatis) An area of the moon's surface, sometimes visible from the earth as a dark spot in the moon's northern hemisphere. *Apollo 11*'s lunar landing module, the *Eagle*, landed in the southwestern part of the Sea of Tranquillity on July 20, 1969.

sheikh Chief or leader of a group of Arabs.

stratosphere A layer of the earth's atmosphere that starts at about 26,000 feet (8 km) above the Poles and about 55,000 feet (17 km) above the equator and extends upward to around 165,000 feet (50 km).

thermal imaging A process for producing an image of an object or area of terrain using a special type of camera that is sensitive to minute differences in the heat that is emitted; an especially useful technique for taking pictures at night or in the absence of light.

transit In astronomy, the passage of a planet across the face of the sun as viewed from the earth.

INDEX